CW00558400

'Malcolm Patten has brought together ha[...] leading of multicultural churches with pro[...] from his careful study of the work of th[...] political and social scientists as well as other church leaders. The result is a book that will be of great assistance to both new and experienced church leaders in multicultural contexts and also to those who seek to understand, encourage and support them.'

The Ven. Dr Andy Jolley, Archdeacon of Bradford

'Multicultural Britain throws up many challenges, not least for the Church whose gospel is that Christ died to create one new humanity. Affirming this in theory is one thing (although sadly not all even do that); bringing it into being in a local church is another. In this book, Dr Patten takes nothing for granted. He presents a biblical survey showing how God's grace embraces everyone and seeks to incorporate all into one people. He then surveys differing contemporary approaches to integration and multiculturalism, before applying this to leading a local church in worship, pastoring, growing other leaders and mission. He often uses his own experience, both failures and achievements, as examples. Among the great values of this book for all ministering in multicultural Britain is its superb and insightful blend of theology, theory and practice. It should be widely read and not just by those in the thick of our multicultural cities, since the issues concern the heart of the gospel and concern us all.'

Dr Derek Tidball, Visiting Scholar at Spurgeon's College, London, and previously Principal of the London School of Theology

'There is no greater joy or challenge in ministry than leading a multi-cultural church. The call of God is to lead, but that leadership can only be truly effective if both the minister and church members are willing to understand and grapple with the tapestry of ethnicities and cultures in their midst, and to do so prayerfully, lovingly and biblically. I did not realize that fully until, like Malcolm Patten, God called me to lead in churches across East London, one of the most richly diverse and exciting areas of our nation. In this book, Malcolm Patten offers well-researched wisdom and insightful reflection from his own experience on this challenge, which create signposts that can only enhance our leadership, whatever the diverse context.'

The Rt Revd Peter Hill, Bishop of Barking

'The United Kingdom in recent years has increasingly become a multicultural society. This brings excitement and challenges for the whole of society and particularly for ministers and churches. This book deals with the issues and challenges of multiculturalism in the Church and provides suggestions and guidelines to lead a successful multicultural church from the author's personal experience of such ministry. The author has also expressed the desire of God rooted in Scripture for church to be of every race, colour, nation, tribe and language, thus leaving us with the missiological challenge to engage with different communities. I believe this resource will be of great inspiration and motivation to church leaders and churches as they continue to minister in the multicultural context.'

The Revd Shahbaz Javed, Walthamstow
United Reformed Asian Church, London

'What do church leaders do when their congregations look like a mini version of the global village? I suggest they reach for this book! Malcolm Patten has chosen a massive topic to address, and I admire his courage. His dream to see our cities full of thriving and relationally functional multi-ethnic churches is one that I commend and equally desire. The book is not always comfortable reading because he is honest about how clumsy we have been at achieving this goal, but there is still hope. Revisiting our concept of churches comprised of members of multi-ethnic origins and the layered culture dynamics present in each group is the place to start a challenging journey. This book should prove a helpful map to get you going in the right direction. These pages contain academic rigour, pastoral transparency and the honesty that tries to yoke them together to make church "do-able" . . . in full technicolor!'

The Revd Douglas C. Williams, Senior Leader of Emmanuel
Community Church International, Walthamstow

'Insightful, packed with wisdom and good ideas. This is an inspiring read for those who desire to grow healthy multicultural church.'

The Revd Rupert Lazar, Minister of East Barnet Baptist Church
and President of the Baptist Union of Great Britain, 2016–17

LEADING A
MULTICULTURAL
CHURCH

Malcolm Patten

First published in Great Britain in 2016

Society for Promoting Christian Knowledge
36 Causton Street
London SW1P 4ST
www.spck.org.uk

Copyright © Malcolm Patten 2016

All rights reserved. No part of this book may be reproduced or transmitted in any form
or by any means, electronic or mechanical, including photocopying, recording,
or by any information storage and retrieval system, without
permission in writing from the publisher.

SPCK does not necessarily endorse the individual views contained in its publications.

The author and publisher have made every effort to ensure that the external website
and email addresses included in this book are correct and up to date at the time
of going to press. The author and publisher are not responsible for
the content, quality or continuing accessibility of the sites.

Unless otherwise noted, Scripture quotations are taken from the Holy Bible,
New International Version (Anglicized edition). Copyright © 1979, 1984, 2011
by Biblica (formerly International Bible Society). Used by permission of Hodder
& Stoughton Publishers, an Hachette UK company. All rights reserved.
'NIV' is a registered trademark of Biblica (formerly International Bible Society).
UK trademark number 1448790.

British Library Cataloguing-in-Publication Data
A catalogue record for this book is available from the British Library

ISBN 978–0–281–07504–1
eBook ISBN 978–0–281–07505–8

Typeset by Graphicraft Limited, Hong Kong
First printed in Great Britain by Ashford Colour Press
Subsequently digitally printed in Great Britain

eBook by Graphicraft Limited, Hong Kong

Produced on paper from sustainable forests

Dedicated to my wife, Maria, and daughter, Anna,
with whom I share the joy of following Jesus every day

Contents

———•◦•———

Contents

Foreword

————◆●◆————

Desperate to rebuild a Britain ravaged by the horrors of the Second World War, the British government called upon the skills and resolve of people from the Caribbean to help resurrect a crumbling economy. On 22 June 1948 the cruise ship *Empire Windrush* docked at Tilbury Dock, Essex. Jamaicans, Trinidadians and other Caribbean islanders walked down the gangplank onto British soil, not imagining that their journeys would prove a turning point in the history of the UK.

The story of Asian migration converged with that of Caribbean. In the face of a struggling workforce, communities from the Indian subcontinent were targeted, recruited and filled numerous job vacancies in the NHS and other organizations. Britain was on its way to becoming a host nation to a wide range of ethnic groups, a process accelerated in 1972 by the expulsion of South Asians from Uganda. Migration from Africa – in particular of West Africans, coming largely as students and business people – increased from the 1990s onwards, and it is impossible to exclude from this growing list the burgeoning numbers of Eastern Europeans entering the UK in recent decades and the vast numbers of vulnerable people seeking sanctuary from war-torn countries. Just like those who came before them, these newer arrivals are exploring ways of belonging to Britain's ever-changing cultural tapestry.

Churches, whether located in the rural suburbs or the sprawling cities, are unable to avoid these tectonic shifts in demographics. These days, it does not matter where the church you serve is situated, the diffusion of minority ethnic groups into large numbers of churches reinforces the need for and importance of this book.

Leading a Multicultural Church is a resourceful companion that can help church leaders do what it says on the tin. There are at least three ways in which this book will prove to be very helpful. First, its contents are reflective of an author who has listened to his congregations before putting pen to paper. Based on his listening, Malcolm Patten has developed helpful theories and strategies to enable church leaders to begin to address some of the obstacles that may prevent a church from becoming a genuine multicultural community. It is a book laden with practical advice and wisdom from an experienced pastor and it will be a supportive friend to any church leader committed to developing a culturally just church.

Second, the book has a helpful biblical underpinning. The chapters on 'Thinking biblically about multicultural church' provide a scriptural and theological rationale for leading such a church. The biblical narratives are extensions of what was incarnate in the person and ministry of Jesus Christ and they bear witness to the barrier-breaking mission of God, reaching a climax in worship where all cultures find freedom of expression and none feel dishonoured. These chapters provide the biblical reasoning why church leaders need to be committed to making God's vision a reality.

Finally, this book is long overdue. For years church leaders have been struggling to find effective ways of developing and leading multicultural churches. There are few programmes or courses available to equip ministers with the skills and competencies required for cultivating a culturally diverse congregation.

And so, in the light of a rapidly changing church landscape, with church leaders needing support in this area, this book is an essential read for those training or currently leading such churches. *Leading a Multicultural Church* is not just an engaging and insightful read, it is also abundant in practical wisdom and strategies, and is a vital resource for every church leader seeking to lead and facilitate a congregation underpinned by the values of justice, mercy and liberation.

The Revd Wale Hudson-Roberts
Racial Justice Advisor
Baptist Union of Great Britain

Acknowledgements

I wish first to acknowledge my friends and colleagues Rupert Lazar and Wale Hudson-Roberts. We met at college, where we dreamed of what a multicultural church might look like, and we have continued to discuss, debate and work towards fulfilling that vision ever since. I continue to appreciate the friendship of Augustine and Confidence Njamnshi, who are like a brother and sister to me and constantly remind me that Africans see things differently. Augustine took me on a grass-roots tour of Cameroon some 15 years ago and helped me to see life through another's eyes, an experience which continues to influence my thinking today.

I am deeply grateful to God for the congregations I have been privileged to serve as minister: Tottenham Baptist Church, where I began and learned so much the hard way; West Croydon Baptist Church, which allowed me to carry out qualitative research within the congregation; and Blackhorse Road Baptist Church, Walthamstow, who have been exceedingly gracious in allowing me a sabbatical to help this book along the way. Many of the illustrations and examples in the book are based on encounters and experiences among these communities.

I am indebted to Spurgeon's College, London for their hospitality and support. The biblical reflections and theoretical material in the book have arisen out of my studies and research there and at times, during the writing of the book, the college has been my second home. It was the staff of Spurgeon's College who encouraged me on various occasions to convert my doctoral thesis into a practical book to serve the Church and it is to their credit that this book is finally seeing the light of day.

In the writing of the book my thanks go to Tracey Messenger, commissioning editor at SPCK, who with her sharp eye and keen mind has undoubtedly improved the book and its usefulness to all who read it, though any remaining errors or weaknesses are mine and mine alone. Many people have been kind enough to discuss parts of the book with me or advise on certain aspects of it. There are too many to mention but the book is the richer for their input. A shorter version of Chapters 2 and 3 appeared in the journal *Evangelical Quarterly* (Vol. 85.3, July 2013) under the title 'Multicultural Dimensions of the Bible', and I remain grateful to the late New Testament scholar I. Howard Marshall for his kind encouragement.

Finally, my wife Maria and daughter Anna have sacrificed family time to allow me to complete my work on the book. Maria has continually encouraged me to 'get on and finish it!', not because she is sick of it, but because she believes it can make a difference. I am immensely grateful for their love and support.

1

Introduction

---•--•--•---

My story

Any discussion in the area of multiculturalism is fraught with vested interests. Who is speaking is as important as what they are saying. So I will begin with my own story, pause to lay my cards down on the table and declare my hand. The deficiencies in what I write will then be evident by the limitations of my experience, but I trust that in sharing what I have learned, it may be useful to many whose experience and journey is different from mine.

I grew up in Hartlepool, in the north-east of England. It is a town with a relatively settled population and until recently its inhabitants were almost entirely of white British origin. I remember two boys at my secondary school who were black, and a family of Vietnamese refugees who moved into a house near my home church. I also remember local youths daubing racist remarks on the refugees' garden fence. In my home church we occasionally had an Asian person join us for a time as he or she worked out a placement at the local hospital. And my parents were the missionary representatives for our church, which meant we often hosted missionaries on home leave as they recounted their adventures in places far away.

When I moved to London to begin my training for the Baptist ministry, my closest friends were fellow students who were British but originated respectively from Trinidad and Tobago and Nigeria. The whole experience of moving to London from the north-east of England and building new friendships with people whose ethnic backgrounds were different from my own opened my eyes and my heart in a new way to the diversity of the world I lived in.

I began my first full-time pastorate as the minister of a Baptist church in north London. The congregation of around 60 people represented a mixture of nationalities, though English and Jamaican people dominated statistically. There were people from other Caribbean countries, from West African countries, in particular Nigeria and Ghana, and from Europe, including Spain, Italy and Ukraine. After nine years I moved to become the associate minister at a larger church in Croydon, a church with a similar ethnic mix to the church in Tottenham but with the added presence of people from countries in Asia such as Pakistan, India and Sri Lanka.

It quickly became evident that the pastoral task in both congregations required a diverse approach for a diverse community. Customs vary greatly between people of different ethnic backgrounds, revealing themselves not only in the arrangement of infant blessings, weddings and funerals, but also in a myriad of ways in general church life. Musical expectations, styles of praying, preaching and leadership all vary from culture to culture. Some people expect a speedy welcome visit when visiting a church for the first time, whereas others are put off by such an immediate intrusion upon their privacy. Concepts of children's work, evangelism and social concern also vary. Contrasting theologies of healing, giving and hospitality can lead to cultural clashes and embarrassment.

Beyond these expressions of difference deeper issues emerged. There was the issue of power in the church: why is the indigenous host community over-represented in the leadership? Is it a problem, and if so, how can the situation be changed? Why does a welcome to the 'stranger' often generate an assumption that the church belongs to one particular ethnic group? In other words, 'I welcome you into my home, but it is still *my* home. I welcome you to my church but it is still *my* church.' Both first-generation immigrants and members of the indigenous host community had lived through significant changes in the ethnic make-up of their community. Yet, I realized, their experiences had never been discussed within the life of their church. People who worshipped together as a church family and had known each other for years had little insight into one another's lives. They had never listened to one another's stories.

There seemed to be a fear of conflict, a concern that if the issues were raised and the differences discussed then it would inevitably lead to disagreement and racism. Nevertheless, my response in both communities was to set about exploring the issues raised in multicultural churches. In Tottenham, a six-week course led by the London Baptist Association's Racial Justice Co-ordinator provided just such an opportunity. Those who joined in shared the pains and joys of their experiences, growing closer to each other and deepening their understanding of their world. A booklet was published by the church containing 13 stories of different people's experiences of living in a multicultural community. On the day of its launch the Mayor of Haringey, himself originally from Guyana, came and spoke at the church; directing his remarks particularly to the black young people in the congregation, encouraging them to pursue education, he thereby demonstrated his own grasp of one of the significant issues of the time.

We also set aside a day for members of the congregation to host meals in their homes with people from differing ethnic backgrounds. This led to a journey of discovery for many as they saw for the first time the different tastes of others, such as their choice of decor, and shared their stories first hand.

When I moved to Croydon it was to join the Trinidadian colleague I had known from college days, in part because we had a common interest in the issues that arise in multicultural churches. We felt a call from God to work together to tackle these issues and explore what it meant to be a multicultural church in the UK. During this time I conducted research among the congregation, asking open-ended questions such as how members of the congregation felt about being part of a multi-cultural church, what they liked or didn't like about it. Some of the quotes and examples in this book come from that period of research. I have changed names and some particulars where necessary to maintain an element of anonymity.

I currently serve as senior pastor of a church in Walthamstow in east London, where the greater Muslim presence in the local community has presented a new challenge but has also given me the opportunity to implement in a fresh context learning points that arose from my earlier research. I am married to Maria, the daughter of Jamaican immigrants, and we have one daughter who delights in her diverse heritage. For the purposes of this book I asked her 'How do you describe yourself?' 'Mixed,' she replied. I asked her whether she thought that was a good thing or a bad thing. 'Good, I like it,' she said. 'Because I have a bit of Jamaican and a bit of Hartlepool in me.' She spends her days at school mixing with young people of many different ethnic, cultural and religious backgrounds. Her church too brings her into contact with a great variety of people and influences. It is with her future in mind that I offer this book.

The purpose of this book

Britain has always had elements of ethnic diversity, but since the 1950s that diversity has increased dramatically. The post-war period saw an influx of people from the Caribbean who were encouraged to work in the UK, many planning to return home after a few years. There are a variety of stories as to how they were received. Some migrants went along to their local church and were welcomed and assisted to settle; many were marginalized yet persisted in attending the established Church. But because of the mixed reception new expatriate churches were planted, places those rejected by the main denominational churches could call their spiritual home.

In the following decades increasing numbers of Africans came to study in the UK as part of the British Commonwealth's endeavour to encourage the economic development of former colonial countries. People from other parts of the world were also finding their way to the UK, particularly in response to conflict or persecution; in the 1970s these included Asian people purged from Uganda and Vietnamese boat people.

Certainly people from the Caribbean and Africa were much more likely to want to attend church than the indigenous British and this has, on reflection, been the saving grace of what otherwise has been a bleak period in the history of the Church in Britain, particularly in its major cities. The loss of confidence and faith as a consequence of the two world wars has in part been mitigated by the enthusiasm and commitment of immigrants who have made the UK their new home. And although there are many examples of racism, many lessons have been learned by the major denominations: a greater awareness of the issues in multicultural congregations has been encouraged, racial justice issues have been addressed and diversity celebrated. We are a long way from where we need to be in these areas but progress has undoubtedly been made.

This book aims to grapple with the situation we find ourselves in now, which has changed again in four significant ways. It has changed first of all because the rate of immigration has increased in recent decades. Between 2001 and 2011 the proportion of people in Britain from ethnic minority backgrounds increased from 13 per cent to 20 per cent. In London, in 2011, over 55 per cent of people were from ethnic minority backgrounds.[1] These demographic changes are reflected in an analysis of the ethnic diversity of church attendance. The English Church Census of 2005 revealed that 83 per cent of churchgoers were white, 10 per cent black, and 7 per cent from other non-white backgrounds; in London, only 42 per cent of churchgoers were white, 44 per cent black and 14 per cent from other non-white backgrounds.[2]

People now migrate to the UK from many different places and so the diversity within churches that are already multicultural has increased further. Whereas there may once have been a relatively small number of recognizable groups within church life (the Jamaicans, the Nigerians, the South Asians), the spread of ethnicities within such congregations is now much wider, including people from central and eastern European countries, China and South America. One of the ways that this has a direct impact on congregations is that whereas migrants from the former British colonies generally spoke English, many new migrants are less proficient in the language, and therefore communication is a much greater problem. The continuing rise of expatriate congregations in a mother tongue bears witness to this.

A second way in which the situation in the UK has changed is that whereas multicultural churches were once mainly found in the major towns and cities, increasingly migrants are settling in towns and villages whose populations have hitherto remained largely indigenous. There are four reasons for this: legislation distributes asylum seekers around the UK once their claim has been received; local councils in the major cities relocate migrant families because of housing shortages; migrant families themselves choose to move out to areas that are more affordable; and migrant families who have grown in affluence choose to move to more desirable areas to live.

The change has come about, third, because those who formed part of earlier migrations have been settled for some time and their children and grandchildren, second- and third-generation migrants, have grown up in Britain. This means that they express their ethnic identity in a variety of ways. Some are keen to maintain strong ties with the customs and traditions of their ancestors, some are much more assimilated into British ways, and many have the ability to foster both aspects of their heritage. Inter-ethnic marriage has also played its part; children of mixed heritage represent the fastest growing 'ethnic minority' and are inherently multicultural in their identity.

The fourth change is that the political environment has become increasingly hostile towards new migrants and many are struggling to make their way in life in the UK. Many encounters between churches and migrants, whether members of those churches' congregations or not, will relate to visa or welfare issues, or will come through refugee support groups and night shelters. There are of course students and professional people who have migrated to the UK and are self-sufficient. But many in our local communities are not, and turn to the Church seeking help and support, sometimes as a last resort.

This book is designed to help church leaders equip themselves to respond to the challenges of leading and shaping a multicultural congregation. It may also help leaders of other Christian organizations, such as colleges and parachurch organizations, navigate with greater confidence and wisdom the changing face of Christianity in Britain. If you have spent any time in a multicultural congregation you will know that it can be both the best of places and the worst of places. It can be a place of celebration, bursting with cultural expressions in dress, food and music, with insights into Scripture and wisdom as to how to resolve problems in church life that you would never have known and an anticipation of the kingdom to come in all its fullness. However it can also be a frustrating place, where trying to please everyone leads to no one being happy and issues of prejudice are never far away.

The shape of this book

The book is in two parts. The first part aims to lay foundations upon which we will build as we go. Chapters 2 and 3 attempt to construct a biblical worldview that will help us as we think about multicultural church, Chapter 2 exploring the Old Testament (OT) and Chapter 3 the New Testament (NT). They will show how the assimilationist approach of the Israelites in the OT gives way to an integrative approach in the NT, allowing for ethnic groups to maintain their customs and cultural ways yet negotiating ways of living together as the unified body of Christ.

Chapter 4 delves briefly into the debates in the public domain over the best way to develop harmonious communities, finding a particular resonance with the approach of the political philosopher Lord Bhikhu Parekh and his call to seek unity without uniformity and to 'cultivate in multicultural communities both a common sense of belonging and a willingness to respect and cherish deep cultural differences' (Parekh, 1999). Chapter 5 addresses the issue of prejudice, and draws on the research and thought of social psychologist Gordon Allport to propose the necessary conditions in church life that will help to overcome prejudice and foster the development of a healthy, growing multicultural church.

Part 2 of the book draws from the principles established in Part 1 and applies them in four different areas of church life: worship, pastoral care, leadership and mission. Although the book aims to help church leaders improve their skill and competency in leading a multicultural church, the nature of the beast is such that multicultural churches are constantly changing and therefore these chapters cannot offer an answer to every situation that may arise. It is hoped, however, that there will be sufficient here to enable any church leader to find resonance with his or her situation, allowing them to discover frameworks and tools to assist them, and to gain encouragement and hope on their particular journey.

Definitions

The preferred terms I shall use in this book are to refer to people of 'differing ethnic backgrounds' and of a 'multicultural' church. Taking each in turn: I prefer to talk of people of 'differing ethnic backgrounds' because it seems to me a more inclusive way to speak of ethnic differences than to talk of black people, BME (Black, minority ethnic), BAME (Black, Asian, minority ethnic) or simply people from a minority ethnic background. Because this book is not focused on the disadvantages of particular groups but on how people of every and any ethnic background can work together for the kingdom of God, I have tried to select a term that excludes no one and assumes the superiority of no particular group. It arguably includes the host ethnic community on the same footing (in descriptive terms) as those that have come to join it. It works, too, for majority black churches and other expatriate churches who are seeking to encourage indigenous British people to feel at home and participate fully in their churches.

With regard to the term 'multicultural' I find that it is still used in common parlance to refer to the presence of people from differing ethnic backgrounds and so I have stuck with it. Others will prefer 'multi-ethnic' or 'intercultural', but within the UK (and apart from academic literature) I find 'multicultural' continues to be the usual word on people's lips and the one used most regularly in the media. It is worth noting at this stage that 'multiculturalism' generally carries a significantly different meaning: it is a term used to describe the task of actively pursuing the development of cultural communities, investing in them and affirming their particular identity without necessarily encouraging interaction between them. This idea is flawed and is something we will discuss further in Chapter 4. However, in church circles the usual understanding of 'multicultural' is the presence and fellowship together of people from differing ethnic backgrounds, and it is in that sense I use it here.

The terms 'race', 'racism' and 'multi-racial' have been avoided as far as possible in the book. This is because 'race', from the sixteenth century, was 'perceived of as a consequence of lineage or descent' and led to the justification of slavery to enable the exploitation of resources in the European colonies, particularly in the USA and Caribbean (Karlsen and Nazroo, 2006, p. 23). Because of this misconception and its consequences it seems inappropriate to continue with its usage. However, this does not in any way negate awareness of the lingering consequences of this flawed philosophy; prejudice and institutional racism are explored in Chapters 5 and 7 respectively.

'Ethnicity' and 'culture' are difficult terms to define with any accuracy, and are fluid in their usage over time. Generally I use 'ethnicity' to describe a person's national or tribal heritage and sense of historical belonging, and 'culture' as a broader and looser description of a person's identity including elements of behaviour and attitudes. So, for example, I am ethnically British and from the north-east of England even though I live in London. Culturally, however, I find myself distanced from some of the traits normally associated with people from the north-east and have accumulated habits, attitudes and preferences that reflect the many years I have spent in a cosmopolitan city. Culturally I also reflect the behaviours and attitudes of someone born in the 1960s and presently in their fifties. This shapes the music I listen to, the television I like to watch and the shared experiences in life I can talk about with others. Ethnicity and culture are, though, also in part attributed by the society a person inhabits, so even though I have lived in London for many years, I am still described by my peers as a 'northerner'.

To give a further example of the contrast between ethnicity and culture, my wife Maria was born in London to Jamaican parents. Ethnically she is of Jamaican origin but is defined by society as black British. Culturally she reflects elements both of Jamaican behaviours and attitudes and those typical of someone who has lived most of her life in north London and moves effortlessly among white Londoners and British Jamaicans, understanding the ways of life of both cultural communities. We shall reflect further on the notion of identity in Chapter 4.

Before we move on from definitions, it is worth observing the distinction between those in our denominations and churches pursuing racial justice and those pursuing the healthy development of multicultural church. The United Reformed Church recognizes the distinction by having a 'Secretary for Racial Justice and Multicultural Ministry'. Racial justice and multicultural ministry are really two approaches to the same issue and I would contend that both are necessary. Racial justice seeks to draw attention to the sins of the past and ongoing injustices in the present, and to confront racism as it manifests itself today. It is negatively focused, with the hope that as people understand and repent then justice will be served and the Church can become more harmonious. Multicultural ministry seeks to envision what church should become as the people of God gathered from many nations, and considers the principles that need to be in place to reach that point. Along the way this necessarily includes an appreciation of what has gone wrong in the past and a better understanding of the history that makes it so difficult to build unity and community. These are distinct ministries but ones that need each other and overlap with each other. Arguably the former, racial justice, starts with the problems of the past and works forward, whereas the latter, multicultural ministry, starts with a vision of the future and works back.

When I was a child I harboured a desire to travel the world. In my ministry I find that I travel the world through the people I meet. Sometimes as we share stories, food and perspectives on life, I feel as though I have been to the places involved myself! These are exciting times as people from all around the world become part of our church community life together. I hope this book proves useful in your own journey as a leader of a multicultural church and helps you to discover not merely the challenges and frustrations, but also the joys and delights that these wonderful diverse communities can bring.

Part 1
LAYING FOUNDATIONS

2

Thinking biblically about multicultural church: Old Testament

The purpose of this chapter and the one that follows is to explore the extent to which the Bible has multicultural dimensions. I shall begin by developing a multicultural hermeneutical approach to interpreting the Bible and then explore multicultural dimensions of the Old and New Testaments respectively, examining both the multicultural texture of the community of God's people and the lessons to be learned from their intercultural encounters. At the end of Chapter 3 I shall outline the contours that emerge in developing a tentative biblical framework for multicultural ministry.

Developing a multicultural hermeneutical approach to interpreting the Bible

It is appropriate, even before we examine the text, to consider how in this context Scripture should be approached and within what framework of understanding we should develop our interpretation. The biblical scholar Chris Wright, in his seminal work *The Mission of God*, writes, 'We live in an age of a multinational church and multidirectional mission. And appropriately we now live with multicultural hermeneutics. People will insist on reading the Bible for themselves, you see' (Wright, 2006, p. 38).

The process of reading Scripture and reflecting on it in one's own context has always been a necessary task of the Christian community. So it follows that within a multicultural community, the task of reflecting on Scripture and discerning its appropriate application requires a multicultural hermeneutic. There are examples, such as the *Africa Bible Commentary*, of efforts to develop ethnic or cultural hermeneutics appropriate for a particular community.[1] The general introduction to that commentary states, 'The Bible needed to be interpreted and explained to the people in familiar language, using colloquial metaphors, African thought-forms and nuances, and practical applications that fitted the African context' (Adeyemo, 2006, p. viii). It is perhaps worth noting that while the *Africa Bible Commentary* is aimed primarily at African heritage believers, it also makes a valuable contribution in multicultural communities in assisting those who are not of African heritage to understand better the worldviews of others in their community when reading or preaching from the Bible.

Wright affirms that his concern to develop a missional hermeneutic must include 'the multiplicity of perspectives and contexts from which and within which people read the biblical texts' (Wright, 2006, p. 39). Nevertheless, in the attempt to develop a multicultural-missional hermeneutic, he is also concerned not to develop one which becomes pluralist or relativist in nature. Rather he aligns himself with James Brownson, an American theologian of the reformed tradition, in striving for a coherent diversity that finds its unity within a salvation-historical reading of Scripture (Wright, 2006, pp. 39–41).[2]

Mission theologian Martha Franks also wrestles with this in the context of developing a missional hermeneutic of Scripture. She writes, 'The great issue connected with mission is how to be true to the faith that we have received, and yet also to present that faith in a way that can be understood and adopted into cultures very different from that in which we received it' (Franks, 1998, p. 333). The context of the present book differs from that considered by Franks, given that she is reflecting on the manner in which the gospel is proclaimed for the first time in cross-cultural situations, whereas my concern is the living out of the gospel in a multicultural context. However, there is a resonance here in the sense that in any congregation, there remains a multiplicity of cultural and ethnic filters through which the Bible is being read and understood.

Franks acknowledges this tendency, drawing on Old Testament scholar Gerhardt von Rad's portrayal of the people of God of the Old Testament evidently evolving their self-understanding and their role in God's purposes over the course of time. Such an observation lends itself to a post-modern approach to Scripture in which 'our text has not only many different voices within it, but also many different meanings for different people' (Franks, 1998, p. 338). She asserts: 'Christian missiology has long preceded the postmodern world in recognizing the possible problem of the fact that transplanting language and concepts from one context to another leads to wholly new ways of understanding them' (Franks, 1998, p. 342). Here Franks investigates the extent to which ethnicity and culture shapes the way the text is, or indeed could be, received and understood. She also touches on an aspect of the multicultural context with regard to what extent ethnicity and culture are intrinsic to human identity, and therefore should and must be allowed to play a part in determining the interpretation. If ethnicity and culture do shape fundamentally who we are and how we act or react in any given situation, then this lends itself to a greater openness to a pluralist hermeneutical approach. The relationship between ethnicity, culture and human identity is something that will arise again in Chapter 4, where Bhikhu Parekh's approach to multiculturalism in society is discussed.

Gambian-born historian and missiologist Lamin Sanneh considers the impact of ethnicity and culture on the interpretation of Scripture from the perspective of Bible translation in mission. In his consideration of the African context for translation he writes:

Scriptural translation pursued the logic that the mother tongue has a primary affinity with the message of the gospel, the point being conceded by the adoption of indigenous terms and concepts for the central categories of the Bible. As long as missionaries were committed to translation, so long would vernacular concepts and usage continue to shape and direct the transmission of Christianity, including the understanding of God by more inclusive criteria.   (Sanneh, 2009, p. 201)

For Sanneh not only is the message of the text of Scripture open to interpretation, but also the actual process of how the text is interpreted is shaped by the context and culture of those receiving it. His statement that 'vernacular concepts and usage continue to shape and direct the transmission of Christianity' suggests that both the message itself and the way it is interpreted, the hermeneutic involved, is affected. However, he goes on to state that the message of Christianity and the understanding of God for the whole of the community of faith becomes fuller and more complete by the facilitation of this process.

By stating that differing ethnic and cultural readings of the Bible will inevitably contribute to a more complete understanding of the Bible for all, Sanneh seeks to develop a relationship between a multicultural approach to interpreting Scripture and the particularist approach taken by those who attempt to interpret Scripture through one specific cultural lens. Thus we return to Wright's question, raised above, of how coherence and fidelity to Scripture are balanced against an increasing plurality of interpretation. To illustrate this using a musical analogy, we may compare an orchestra playing classical music with a jazz ensemble. In the orchestra the musicians will play their parts exactly as written, with little room for variation from the original score. They will anticipate that any other orchestra will play the piece more or less in the same way. The quality of the tone and expression is all that is left open for interpretation. The jazz ensemble, however, will take an original melody and within the contours of the piece allow each instrument to improvise in its own particular way, discovering new breadth and depth to the music and presenting it uniquely on each occasion that it is played. The jazz ensemble will anticipate that any other ensemble may well develop the music in ways they had not thought of. The music remains an expression of the original score, but the jazz ensemble takes us on a journey to discover it afresh in ways previously unimagined.

The interpretation of Scripture within any one particular culture will thus be similar to the orchestral approach to music, with little variation. It is when Scripture is interpreted within a fresh cultural worldview that new dimensions of interpretation and expression begin to take shape, challenging and enriching those that we have previously been familiar with.

An example of an attempt at a multicultural approach to Scripture can be found in theologian Timothy Tennent's discussion of atonement in shame-based cultures. He states, 'Anthropologists have consistently observed that the concept of shame and the maintenance of public honour is one of the "pivotal values" outside the West' (Tennent, 2007, p. 78). By showing how shame-based cultures can be contrasted with the guilt-based cultures which are widely accepted to predominate in the Western world, Tennent demonstrates how a deepening appreciation for this aspect of atonement can unfold new dimensions of interpretation within a Western worldview, representing in terms of our metaphor a variation on the theme of the music. The result is a more textured, inclusive approach to interpretation of Scripture which serves the Church globally and becomes a challenging and enriching element of our continuing journey with Scripture. Such an approach is increasingly necessary in a diverse Church (Tennent, 2007, p. 101).

This balance between maintaining the coherence of doctrine and making space for ethnic and cultural interpretations is, however, tested by, for example, the Jamaican post-colonialist theologian Noel Erskine. Having described the dominant (Western) theology as colonial theology, he writes, 'One of the emphases of colonial theology was on individual salvation . . . Black religion began the process of decolonizing theology when it insisted that God was the freeing one, who was at work in history setting the victims free' (Erskine, 1998, pp. 167–8). Here the tension between the theology of the Reformers and liberation theology emerges – an emphasis on individual salvation by grace against an emphasis on salvation expressed as political and social transformation. This is not a new issue, having showed itself throughout much of the twentieth century in the form of the debates between evangelicals and liberals, but it presents itself in a new way in the context of the global Church.

British theologian and missiologist Andrew Walls attempts some conciliation of the issue when he writes,

> There are not different gospels for individuals and for society. There is no question of there being an option of which to pro-claim, or of balancing the claims of one against another. Nor are there different gospels for different kinds of people, or for different situations. There is only one good news of salvation through Jesus Christ, resting on one event, the death and resur-rection of the divine Son. But the scope of that event, and of the gospel on which it rests, is beyond the most comprehensive description of it as experienced by any person or by any part of the redeemed creation . . . And since the application of the good news is greater than anyone's experience of it, we may well proclaim the good news in anticipation of a response reflecting our own experience; we find others responding in quite another way, but nevertheless hearing good news. For at every level at which the good news is heard, it corresponds with reality, with a real victory secured by Christ over the forces of evil and death.   (Walls, 2002, p. 20)

With Walls's words in mind, it will suffice here to imagine the development of a multicultural hermeneutic which will facilitate a variety of interpretations and understandings while allowing for variation in the manner in which interpretation evolves. Indeed, a multicultural (in contrast to a cross-cultural) hermeneutic will of necessity be mainly concerned to discern the multicultural texture and shape of and the cross-cultural encounters within the Bible, irrespective of how they apply to any one particular ethnic group or culture, while differing cultures may well highlight different aspects or bring deeper or clearer understanding to the biblical text. Bearing this in mind we shall now turn to explore the Bible itself.

Multicultural dimensions of the Old Testament

The creation of diversity and the origins of Israel

Before the emergence of Abraham and his family it is already affirmed in the Bible that the existence of a diversity of people and people groups is intrinsic to the plan and purpose of God. This is reflected in Genesis 1—11, culminating in the Table of Nations in chapter 10 and the scattering of nations in chapter 11. In Genesis 10 we find that 70 nations are the product of Noah's three sons and that these are all offspring of Noah himself, thereby facilitating a sense of common humanity (Hamilton, 1990, p. 346). OT scholar Horst Preuss points out that according to Genesis 10, 'Israel enjoys vis-à-vis the nations no pre-eminence due to creation, mythology or prehistory' (Preuss, 1996, p. 285).[3] Another OT scholar, Claus Westermann, concurs, stating, 'God is the creator of all humankind. God created the whole human race – this statement is spelled out in detail, as it were, by the Table of Nations at the end of the Primal History: the human race, which exists today as a multiplicity of nations, is the human-ity created by God' (Westermann, 2004, p. 79).

It is important to go back a step at this point and consider the issue of what has been known as the 'curse of Ham', derived from Genesis 9.18–27. Noah becomes drunk and lies uncovered inside his tent. Ham sees his father naked and tells his brothers, Shem and Japheth, who subsequently take a garment and lay it over Noah without seeing his nakedness. However, when Noah awakes, he is angry that his younger son Ham has seen him naked and declares, 'Cursed be Canaan! The lowest of slaves will he be to his brothers' (Genesis 9.25).

This curse has been of grave concern for black people in the West. The significance of the story for us is that Ham was seen as the ancestor of black people and that the transatlantic slave trade of the eighteenth and nineteenth centuries was justified, biblically, in part because of a distorted reading of this text. It was argued that black people were destined to be slaves because of the curse upon Ham and his descendants. It seems incredible to us today that such a distortion could take place, but theologian Daniel Hays outlines three reasons how it came about: first, the curse was subtly shifted from Canaan to Ham; second, Ham means 'black' or 'burnt'; and third, God pronounced that Ham's descendants be slaves to those of Shem and Japheth, who were perceived respectively to be the ancestors of the Israelites and Europeans (Hays, 2003, pp. 51–2).

OT scholar Victor Hamilton agrees with Hays in disputing the above, distorted, interpretation of the Noah story; he makes the point that the curse is in fact directed to Canaan and the blessing is not on Shem but towards the God of Shem (Hamilton, 1990, p. 325). Hamilton, like OT theologian Walter Brueggemann, understands the passage to be political rather than genetic. As Brueggemann states, 'This narrative is an opportunity to root in pre-history the power relations between Israel and Canaan and to justify it on theological grounds' (Brueggemann, 1982). Hamilton concurs, but from a different perspective: 'In effect it outlines future history, when Israel conquered Canaan and the Sea Peoples were carving out their own niche in Canaanite-held lands' (Hamilton, 1990, p. 327). Hays says, 'The curse on Canaan, therefore, should be interpreted within the Old Testament context and identified with the victory of the Israelites over the Canaanite inhabitants of the Promised Land. It is incorrect to call this the "curse of Ham", or to identify it with Black Africa or Africans in any way' (Hays, 2003, p. 56).

As can be seen, the trend of biblical scholarship moved away long ago from what was an anachronistic and indeed racist approach of interpreting Genesis 9.18–27, but it is still a view well known among older black Christians and remains an example of how an inappropriate reading of Scripture can lead to a distortion of both the way the text is understood and the way it is applied in a particular context or towards a particular people group.

If Genesis 10 and the Table of Nations represent the fulfilment of the command of God to Noah to be fruitful and increase to fill the earth, the arrogant gathering of the people with one language and the building of the Tower of Babel in Genesis 11 marks their resistance to obeying that command and comes as a problem to be resolved (Wenham, 1987, p. 242). On the one hand the building of the Tower of Babel reflects humanity's pride and is subject to judgement (Wenham, 1987, p. 245); on the other the scattering of the nations as a consequence represents the assertion of God that diversity is within his purpose. In this vein OT scholar Bernhard Anderson draws two conclusions from his discussion of the Tower of Babel text: first, that God's will for his creation is diversity rather than homogeneity; second, that despite this, human beings 'strive for unity and fear diversity' (Anderson, 1994, p. 177). Certainly human beings like to be with people with whom they share familiar traits, and to be thrown into a diverse environment can be disorientating for them. The tension between a diverse humanity that has its source in a creative God, and human beings with their desire to be with others like themselves in a familiar sameness, is one which will resonate throughout this book.

Such an affirmation of diversity is evident in the ethnic and cultural origins of Israel. From Genesis 11.28, 31 and 12.1 we find that Abraham was urged by the call of God to migrate from Ur in Mesopotamia via Haran to Canaan. Ur was in the part of the world known today as Iraq. At the time it was dominated by the Sumerians, described as the 'black-headed' ones, a term believed to refer not only to the colour of their hair but also to their skin (Felder, 1991, p. 154). They formed a highly civilized society and had a significant cultural and linguistic impact on their world, including Israel. The Old Testament scholar John Bright says of this people group that their 'metal working and gem-cutting reached heights of excellence seldom surpassed ... Trade and cultural contacts reached far and wide' (Bright, 1981, p. 34).

There were also Semites and Arameans in the region. The Arameans are of particular interest as it seems that Abraham was predominantly of Aramean origin (Deuteronomy 26.5).[4] Like the Arameans, he was a pastoralist (Van De Mieroop, 2004, p. 192), and the story of Jacob's flight to Aram shows that Abraham's daughter-in-law was Aramean. However, Bright goes on to say, 'There is no evidence of racial or cultural conflict. We may not doubt that an increasing intermingling of the races took place' (Bright, 1981, p. 36). William Schniedewind, an expert in this field, concurs, stating that 'the Aramean states arose from ethnically diverse, semi-nomadic peoples' (Schniedewind, 2002, p. 276). So from whichever ethnic group Abraham emerged to found the people of Israel, it is reasonable to say that his context was multicultural, dominated by the Sumerians.

The call of God to Abraham to be a blessing to all nations of the world will be examined in the next section of this chapter, but continuing our investigation of Israel's ethnic origins leads to consideration of the ethnic constitution of Israel when leaving Egypt under the leadership of Moses. They had journeyed to Egypt as a large extended family but emerged from Egypt a nation. Moreover, they left Egypt having increased the diversity of their ethnic heritage. Joseph had been given a new Egyptian name by Pharaoh and a wife named Asenath, who herself was the daughter of an Egyptian priest (Genesis 41.45). Von Rad observes that as a result, 'Joseph has become completely Egyptian' (Von Rad, 1972, p. 379), although Hamilton notes that he gave Hebrew names to his two sons, Ephraim and Manasseh, who later became fathers to two of the tribes of Israel (Hamilton, 1995, p. 512). Glenn Usry and Craig Keener point out that this means Israel as a people group had subsequently nearly 10 per cent Egyptian heritage. The complexion of ancient Egyptians we know from art to have been a variety of shades from brown through to black, and so we can assert that at least two of the tribes of Israel are likely to have had significant colouring and a mixed ethnic heritage (Usry and Keener, 1996, p. 73).

Furthermore, Egypt was not in itself mono-ethnic. In particular it had a close relationship with the Upper Nile, drawing on the Nubian region for workers at every social level right down to (and including) slaves. The Nubian people included the Cushites (who were black and negroid in appearance), one of whom subsequently married Moses as his second wife.[5] When Israel emerged as a nation desperate to leave Egypt, they did not leave alone. There were other oppressed people who wanted to leave with them (Exodus 12.38). Brueggemann makes the point that 'earliest Israel was not an ethnic community, but a sociological grouping of the marginated [*sic*] who had been liberated from their oppressed socioeconomic status' (Brueggemann, 1994, p. 781). It may be that Brueggemann overstates the case in the light of the detailed instructions for sojourners and foreigners (discussed below), which imply that there was at least some demarcation between those who obviously 'belonged' and those who did not. However it seems clear that the people group leaving Egypt was broader than merely the biological descendants of Abraham (Hays, 2003, p. 68).

This line of argument is further supported by the fact that 'Eleazar son of Aaron married one of the daughters of Putiel, and she bore him Phinehas' (Exodus 6.25). Phinehas is an Egyptian term used to refer to people from Cush. It literally means 'the Nubian' or 'the Cushite' (Durham, 1987, p. 81). Putiel too is an Egyptian name, and the likelihood is that one of Aaron's sons married an Egyptian of Nubian origin and fathered Phinehas. The Bible later affirms that Phinehas became greatly esteemed in the sight of God, an indication that foreigners who joined with the people of Israel were fully accepted (Psalm 106.30–31).

The embracing of all nations and their future hope

The call of Abraham in Genesis 12 was accompanied by a promise that not only would he and his offspring be blessed by God, but 'all peoples on earth will be blessed through you' (Genesis 12.3). We have noted above that the diversity of nations was affirmed and reaffirmed by God; it is made explicit here that the blessing of all nations on earth is the intention, even as one family, which will become the nation of Israel, is favoured to accomplish this end. The relationship between Israel as the elect people of God, and God's intention for all nations, is presented by OT theologian Robin Routledge in terms of centripetal and centrifugal universalism (Routledge, 2008, pp. 326–7).[6] Centripetal universalism relates to those scriptures which refer to the people of other nations being drawn into the people of Israel. An example would be Isaiah 2.3: 'Many peoples will come and say, "Come, let us go up to the mountain of the LORD, to the temple of the God of Jacob. He will teach us his ways, so that we may walk in his paths".'[7] Centrifugal universalism relates to those scriptures which refer to the people of other nations worshipping the God of Israel within their own land. An example would be Malachi 1.11: 'My name will be great among the nations, from where the sun rises to where it sets. In every place incense and pure offerings will be brought to me . . .'[8]

Brueggemann goes a step further than Routledge in his discussion of the people of other nations. Drawing attention to Amos 9.7: ' "Are not you Israelites the same to me as Cushites?" declares the LORD. "Did I not bring Israel up from Egypt, the Philistines from Caphtor and the Arameans from Kir?" ' he states, 'What happens in this striking assertion is that Israel's monopoly on Yahweh is broken. This does not deny that Israel is the primal recipient of Yahweh's powerful, positive intervention, but it does deny any exclusive claim' (Bruggemann, 1997, pp. 520–1).

Brueggemann also draws attention to Isaiah 19.24–25: 'In that day Israel will be the third, along with Egypt and Assyria, a blessing on the earth. The Lord Almighty will bless them, saying, "Blessed be Egypt my people, Assyria my handiwork, and Israel my inheritance".' He comments:

> It is remarkable that the utterance [of Isaiah 19] pertains to the two most despised and perhaps cruelest enemies of Israel . . . The promise is an invitation to Israel to move beyond itself and its self-serving ideology, to reposition itself in the family of beloved nations, and to reimagine Yahweh, beyond any self-serving, privileged claim, into the largest possible horizon, as the one who intends well-being for all the nations.
>
> (Brueggemann, 1997, p. 522)

The focus in second Isaiah on the servant of God draws attention to the anticipation of the 'servant' becoming a light to the Gentiles and by so doing becoming the agent of reconciliation between Israel and the other nations (Isaiah 42.6; 49.6; 52.10). Added to this, third Isaiah portrays the nations coming to Mount Zion, anticipating the fulfilment of the eschatological hope (Isaiah 56.3–8; 60.1–22; 61.5–7). Wright describes this prophetic anticipation as a 'glorious evocation for all the senses of the worship of the nations being brought to YHWH, through the mediation of Israel now functioning, as intended, as God's priesthood for the nations' (Wright, 2006, p. 487).

The theme of the nations praising the God of Israel echoes throughout the Psalms. Wright suggests four reasons the praise of the nations will occur: 'in response to his mighty acts' (Psalms 66; 68; 86; 96—99); 'in response to the justice of his sovereign cosmic rule' (Psalms 2; 22; 67); 'in response to his restoration of Zion' (Psalm 102); and 'as part of the outpouring of the universal praise of all creation' (Psalms 145; 148) (Wright, 2006, pp. 478–84).

Looking more closely at one psalm in particular reveals more clearly the relationship between Israel and the other nations in terms of its partial fulfilment and eschatological hope. Psalm 87 says:

> He has founded his city on the holy mountain. The Lord loves the gates of Zion more than all the other dwellings of Jacob. Glorious things are said of you, city of God: 'I will record Rahab and Babylon among those who acknowledge me – Philistia too, and Tyre, along with Cush – and will say, "This one was born in Zion."' Indeed, of Zion it will be said, 'This one and that one were born in her, and the Most High himself will establish her.' The Lord will write in the register of the peoples: 'This one was born in Zion.' As they make music they will sing, 'All my fountains are in you.'[9]

Commentators differ on what they think the context of this psalm is. Marvin Tate describes an accurate placing of the psalm as elusive and interprets it as a vision of what is to come, it being 'a declaration of God's intention to make Zion the spiritual metropolis of the world' (Tate, 1990, p. 392). He perceives the vision being carried through into the New Testament, with the Gentiles who believe becoming fellow heirs with the Jews of the promises of God, and quotes Hebrews 12.22: 'You have come to Mount Zion, to the city of the living God, the heavenly Jerusalem'. James Mays understands the writer to be referring to Jews who had dispersed from Israel and were living in the different countries mentioned. In this way the psalm is being read as an encouragement to the diaspora that they truly belong to the people of God. Though their descendants were born in another place, it is as if they were born in Zion because of their faith (Mays, 1994, p. 281). Artur Weiser offers a third approach, describing the Temple of Jerusalem during a pilgrimage festival where the writer of the psalm observes a procession of people from all over the world passing by and singing the hymns:

> It is as if the whole world had arranged to meet in this place. They have come from the Nile and the Euphrates, from the lands of the Philistines and of the Phoenicians, and even black figures from distant Ethiopia are not absent from this gathering of nations in the house of God on Mount Zion. However much they may differ from each other in language and appearance, they are all united in one faith.   (Weiser, 1962, p. 580)

It is evident that whichever interpretation of the psalm is preferred, whether an eschatological hope, reassurance for a Jewish diaspora, or a celebration of a reality there and then, the thrust remains the same: that the vision of God for Israel is that of an international, and therefore multicultural, community drawn to worship him.

Summarizing this section, an inclusive instinct is evident here that resonates from the origins of humanity as described in Genesis through the calling of a particular people group through which – and, if Brueggemann is right, alongside which – all nations shall be ultimately blessed under the sovereignty of the God of Israel. This affirmation of people of all nations is an important biblical and theological foundation.

The assimilation of people of other nations within Israel

Legal provisions for assimilation

It has already been shown that a mixed multitude left Egypt with the people of Israel. The presence of these people is particularly evident in that specific instructions were given as to how they should be accommodated within the newly instituted regulations for the Passover outlined in Exodus 12.43–49. Within these regulations two categories of foreigner are described.[10] The first, in Exodus 12.43, is named in the Hebrew as the *nekhar*. Jewish OT scholar Nahum Sarna describes the *nekhar* as the foreigner to Israel 'who resides in the land temporarily, usually for purposes of commerce' (Sarna, 1991, p. 63). Such a person or people group is not expected to want to settle permanently. The second category of foreigner is referred to in Exodus 12.48 in the Hebrew as the *ger*. Sarna notes that the *ger* in Israel 'enjoyed numerous rights and privileges, such as the benefits of the Sabbath rest, the protection afforded by the cities of refuge, and access to a share of certain tithes and to the produce of the Sabbatical year' (Sarna, 1991, p. 64). Both the *nekhar* and the *ger* are instructed not to participate in the Passover unless all the males in their household have covenanted with the people of Israel through the rite of circumcision. However, if they do, then 'he may take part like one born in the land' (Exodus 12.48). It is important to note here the establishing of circumcision of the males as the criterion for belonging which will find its corollary as baptism in the early Church.

Deuteronomy 23 is also of interest here. In verses 3–8, Jewish commentator Jeffrey Tigay notes, certain nationalities are listed as being unable to 'enter the assembly of the Lord', that is the governing assembly of the Israelites and therefore a representation of citizenship (Tigay, 1996, p. 210). This seems to suggest a tightening of the rules for admission to citizenship, raising the question of when this part of Deuteronomy was written and whether it reflects a change of view over time. In other words, was there a consistent view throughout the history of Israel in the OT as to how outsiders could belong, or did the process and ease of belonging vary according to changing circumstances?

Commentator Ronald Clements supports the view that Deuteronomy in its present form was most likely written during the exile and that it reflects the need for a response to the political and religious crisis of that time (Clements, 1998, p. 280).[11] He states, 'what had no doubt earlier been varied and uncoordinated conventions needed to be fixed within a single set of rules' (Clements, 1998, p. 460). What is significant here is the listing of those nationalities which are excluded, which implies that others could be included, and this is made explicit regarding the third-generation Edomites and Egyptians whose descendants can indeed aspire to full citizenship.[12]

Acquiring citizenship also implies the right to marry. Inter-ethnic marriage in Israel raises difficulties, as on the one hand there are notable inter-ethnic marriages, such as those between Moses and the Cushite woman (Numbers 12.1) and Boaz and Ruth the Moabite (Ruth 4.10), yet on the other hand there are also prohibitions. For example in Deuteronomy 7.3, referring to the 'seven nations' inhabiting the land of Canaan, the instruction when the Israelites enter to take possession is clear: 'Do not intermarry with them. Do not give your daughters to their sons or take their daughters for your sons.' The reason given is that 'they will turn your children away from following me to serve other gods'. It seems reasonable to suppose here that the prohibition on marrying those of other nations is related to the danger of syncretism. However, more difficult to understand is the occasion when the exiles return to Judah from Babylon and Ezra leads a purge on the foreign women and their children (Ezra 10). According to Tigay, 'One of the reasons why Ezra, Nehemiah, and their associates demanded the dissolution of intermarriages is that they saw no other way to comply with the law as they understood it.' He goes on to say,

> There is evidence that some of their contemporaries felt that foreigners could be accepted. In Babylonia, there were foreigners who 'attached themselves to the Lord' and served Him, and the prophet of the exile assured them of acceptance. Eventually, this attitude prevailed and procedures for religious conversion were created. (Tigay, 1996, p. 479)

Tigay sees the response in Ezra and Nehemiah as a generalizing of the law in Deuteronomy 23 in response to the circumstances prevailing at that time. Biblical scholar Matthew Thiessen sees it as a legitimate exclusivist radical approach to the issue: 'Israel was the holy seed, all other nations were common seed, and

31

the two were not to be mixed' (Thiessen, 2009, p. 79). It seems likely that there was a variation over time and in response to differing circumstances of the rules of inclusion into the assembly of Israel, but that these rules were tightened and enforced during the exilic and post-exilic periods.

It becomes clear that despite Israel's vocation to be a witness and a blessing to other nations, there remained a fear of syncretism. It is important to acknowledge this variance, while maintaining the principle that despite its desire to maintain its clearly defined boundaries, Israel was still able to facilitate room within those boundaries for those who would identify with its God.

Assimilation on the basis of covenant

Alongside the rules evident in Deuteronomy 23, Ezra and Nehemiah, there is also evidence in the Old Testament of those who assimilated into Israel on the basis of covenant. By this is meant not something of the same dimension as the covenants of Noah, Abraham or David as such, but rather a promise rooted in this fundamental covenantal concept but more locally applied.

In the book of Joshua, Rahab the prostitute is saved from the destruction of Jericho because of her support of the Israelites (Joshua 6.25). The basis of her salvation is not legal but covenantal. She pleads, 'please swear to me by the Lord that you will show kindness to my family, because I have shown kindness to you' (Joshua 2.12). OT theologian Gordon McConville points out that the Hebrew word translated 'kindness' is *hesed*, which is 'the specific quality of covenantal relationship' (McConville, 2010, p. 17). He goes on to assert, 'The standard of being truly "Israel" in Joshua remains covenantal' (McConville and Williams, 2010, p. 35).[13]

Ruth provides a further example whereby a person of another nationality not only assimilates within Israel but in fact marries an Israelite. The basis for this assimilation is the covenant-like commitment of Ruth to Naomi: 'Your people will be my people and your God my God' (Ruth 1.16). The outcome of Ruth's commitment to Naomi is to be taken in marriage by Boaz; consequently she becomes grandmother to King David. Ruth's nationality as a Moabite is no barrier in this context to the transaction taking place and it reflects assimilation into the Israelite community on the basis of covenant rather than law.

Isaiah 56 expresses the reality of a covenant between individual members of other nations and the God of Israel in its affirmation:

> 'Let no foreigner who is bound to the LORD say, "The LORD will surely exclude me from his people." ... foreigners who bind themselves to the LORD to minister to him, to love the name of the LORD, and to be his servants ... these I will bring to my holy mountain and give them joy in my house of prayer ... for my house will be called a house of prayer for all nations.'
>
> (Isaiah 56.3, 6, 7)

OT scholar Brevard Childs rejects the notion that this chapter emerges out of the context of the tightening of regulations in the post-exilic attempt to exclude people of other nations from joining with Israel, but rather sees it as an older text representing an earlier, more open tradition. Crucially, however, he views it in the main from an eschatological perspective, prophesying what is still to come (Childs, 2001, pp. 457–9). In this vein Jesus quotes Isaiah 56.7 when he overturns the tables in the Gentiles' court at the Temple in Jerusalem and refuses to allow any other merchandisers to pass through (Mark 11.15–17). James Jones, a former Bishop of Liverpool, speaks with passion regarding the event:

> I happen to believe that the cleansing of the temple has been misunderstood for centuries. I happen to believe that the cleansing of the temple was not a statement against commercialism but a statement against racism. Jesus said, quoting the Old Testament, 'My house shall be a house of prayer for all races, but you have made it a den of robbers.' Our expositors have concentrated on the 'den of robbers' overlooking the principal

point of Jesus' action which was that His house of prayer should be a house of prayer for 'all' races. It's not what they were doing at the temple but where they were doing it which was the issue.[14]

NT scholar Dick France is sceptical regarding the likelihood of this as a primary interpretation of the passage, arguing that those who would make most use of the area concerned would be Gentiles who had not yet been fully proselytized to Judaism, though he concedes that 'it is not inappropriate that Mark, with an eye to his Gentile readers, has included this part of the Isaiah quotation' (France, 2002, p. 445). NT theologian William Lane points to the significance of the fact that although there are other references in the Old Testament to the Temple as a house of prayer, the clause 'for all nations' occurs only in Isaiah 56.7 and in Mark's quotation of it. Lane argues that Jesus is holding the priestly authorities responsible, not so much accusing them of corruption as indignantly seeking to make possible 'the worship of the Gentiles at the feast of the Passover which commemorated God's redemption of his people' (Lane, 1974, p. 407). In this sense Jesus is signalling continuity with the stream throughout Scripture that all the nations will share in the eschatological fulfilment of that which Isaiah foresaw (Williamson, 1983, p. 207).

3

Thinking biblically about multicultural church: New Testament

———————•◦•———————

Having considered the multicultural dimensions of the Old Testament, we now turn to explore five aspects of the New Testament: the multicultural context of the NT world; cross-cultural encounters in the Gospels; multicultural dimensions of the early Church; multicultural dimensions in the theology of the Apostle Paul; and the vision of a multicultural heaven in Revelation. This chapter concludes by drawing out from Chapters 2 and 3 four biblically based principles which will form a framework to shape our thinking about multicultural church.

The multicultural context of the New Testament world

During the first century BC the Romans subdued much of what had been Alexander's Greek empire, yet inherited its Greek culture. The Greco-Roman world, the political context for the New Testament, was predominantly Hellenistic (Greek) in language and culture, polytheistic in its religion and multi-ethnic in its social constituency.

Faced with the dominance of Greek culture and Roman rule, the Jews living in Palestine tended to become increasingly protective of their own culture and customs. They separated themselves from the prevailing culture yet maintained a strong allegiance with Jews living outside Palestine. This is evident from Acts 2, where Jews from 15 countries are listed as being among those who visit Jerusalem for the feast of Pentecost. Even within Palestine the province of Galilee was run under a separate administration from Judea and the Galileans were looked down upon by the Judeans. The more conservative Jewish areas, such as Nazareth and Capernaum, 'stood in close proximity to largely pagan cities, of which in the first century the new Hellenistic centres of Tiberias and Sepphoris were the chief examples' (France, 2007, p. 6).

What is also evident is that there were significant numbers of people from different people groups (Gentiles) living in, or passing through, Palestine at this time. The Ethiopians (who originated from the area known in the Old Testament period as Cush and in today's world located in the Republic of Sudan) were the traders between the Roman world and sub-Saharan Africa (Hays, 2003, p. 148). Yet they also had goods from their own territory to trade, valuable commodities such as gold, slaves, leopard skins and incense (Yamauchi, 2004, p. 165). They were familiar with the region; in Acts 8.27 'an Ethiopian eunuch, an important official in charge of all the treasury of the Kandake' visits Jerusalem to worship, perhaps while on some diplomatic mission.

North Africans, as they would be described today, also frequented Palestine. They spoke a language akin to ancient Egyptian, strange to the ears of the other ethnic groups settled in Palestine, and thus they acquired the name 'Berbers' – a derivative of barbarian, a term of contempt used for those of strange speech (Colossians 3.11). There were Greek and Roman settlements in North Africa and their inhabitants integrated and intermarried; they exhibited a variety of skin colours, though generally deeper and darker than those found in North Africa today. This is because the Arabic movement into the region came some time after the biblical period (Hays, 2003, p. 151). Simon, from Cyrene in North Africa, was compelled by the Roman soldiers to carry the cross of Jesus (Matthew 27.32), while Cyreneans also congregated in Antioch after the persecution of the Christians which followed the death of Stephen, and occupied key leadership roles in the life of the early Church (Acts 11.20; 13.1).

Pictorial interpretations of biblical stories in the UK have, in the past, often portrayed the characters as if they had the skin colour of western Europeans, perhaps with a beard, long hair and Middle Eastern clothes. Although these pictures demonstrate a self-reflection of Western ethnicity and culture into the biblical narrative, and therefore give a distorted image of reality, ancestors of white Westerners do enter the biblical world in around 280 BC. Gauls from northern Europe poured into Asia Minor and were able to establish the province of Galatia (McEvedy, 2002, p. 78). This was an area the Apostle Paul frequented during the expansion of the early Church (Acts 16.6).

Cross-cultural encounters in the Gospels

Although Jesus draws together 12 disciples who are Jewish and in so doing reflects a continuity of tradition with the 12 tribes of Israel, in many other ways the Gospels reflect Jesus as the Messiah not only for Israel but for the Gentiles too, and therefore continue the theme evident in the Old Testament of God's blessing being for people of all nations (LaGrand, 1999, p. 108). Here we will draw on a selection of passages from each Gospel to demonstrate how they anticipate a widening of the circle from Israel to include people from every nation.

In Matthew's Gospel the opening genealogy includes the four 'mothers': Tamar, Rahab, Ruth and Bathsheba (Matthew 1.3, 5, 6). Hays points out that Sarah and Rebekah were respected matriarchs who could have been chosen if Matthew's purpose for including them was to include women. Noting that Tamar and Rahab were Canaanites, Ruth a Moabite and Bathsheba had been married to Uriah the Hittite, Hays concludes that 'The inclusion of these Gentile women in the lineage would have been shocking to most Jewish readers' (Hays, 2003, p. 159). France states that 'the four "foreign" women prepare the reader for the coming of non-Israelites to follow Israel's Messiah which will be foreshadowed in the homage of the magi in 2.1–12 and will be a recurrent and increasing theme throughout the gospel until it reaches its climax in the mission to all nations in 28.19' (France, 2007, p. 37).[1] He goes on to say: 'This new international community will be his *ekklesia* (16.18)' (France, 2007, p. 1108).

In Mark's Gospel, the event which shows most clearly God's mission to the nations is the cleansing of the Temple (Mark 11.15–17), which has been discussed above, highlighting Jesus' quote from Isaiah 56.7. Mark, alone among the Gospel writers, includes the phrase 'for all nations', emphasizing his interpretation of what Jesus was doing. Lane comments, 'The importance of this would not be lost upon Mark's readers in the predominantly Gentile Church of Rome' (Lane, 1974, p. 407).

As Hays notes, Luke highlights the significance of the gospel being for all nations by linking his theology firmly to the theme of Abraham and the blessing for all nations (Hays, 2003, p. 161). At the presentation of Jesus in the Temple Simeon declares him to be 'a light for revelation to the Gentiles, and the glory of your people Israel' (Luke 2.30–32). Later in Luke's story Jesus demonstrates such openness to non-Jews by recognizing faith in the Roman centurion whose servant he has healed (Luke 7.9). Wright acknowledges Jesus' use of the centurion's faith 'as an opportunity to point to the eschatological hope of the ingathering of the nations to the messianic banquet in the kingdom of God' (Wright, 2006, p. 507).

In John's Gospel Jesus reaches out to the Samaritan woman by the well (John 4). Given the animosity between Jews and Samaritans that is clearly reflected in the text, it is remarkable that Jesus and his disciples spend two days enjoying the hospitality of the Samaritan village (John 4.40), demonstrating Jesus' personal commitment to crossing cultural boundaries. In its context, Jesus' journey in John 2—4, from Jerusalem to Judea, to Samaria and then up to Galilee to encounter a royal official reflects the theme of Acts 1.8: 'and you will be my witnesses in

Jerusalem, and in all Judea and Samaria, and to the ends of the earth'. Theologian and NT commentator Don Carson, commenting on John 4.42, notes: 'It was appropriate that the title "Saviour of the world" should be applied to Jesus in the context of ministry to Samaritans, representing the first cross-cultural evangelism, undertaken by Jesus himself and issuing in a pattern to be followed by the church' (Carson, 1991, p. 232).

Multicultural dimensions of the early Church

The coming of the Holy Spirit on the day of Pentecost, recorded in Acts 2, represents the beginning of the establishment of an international church that was anticipated by the Old Testament and the Gospels. That the message preached was heard in the native languages of those gathered was a miracle in itself. David Peterson sums it up:

> For one brief moment of time, the divisions in humanity expressed through language difference were overcome . . . communication actually took place through the diversity of languages represented there. God was expressing his ultimate intention to unite people 'from every tribe and language and people and nation'.
>
> (Peterson, 2009, p. 136)

There are allusions in Acts 2 to Genesis 11 and the Tower of Babel, referred to above: humanity, which had been dispersed by God in a repudiation of their pride and an affirmation of diversity, is here and now united by a common hearing of the gospel.[2] Unity (though not uniformity) is evident amid diversity as the new community of God's people is established.

Ethnic and cultural issues were to test this unity, so in Acts 6 the apostles are required to solve the problem of the Greek-speaking Jewish widows being neglected in the distribution of food. But the thrust of Acts is the continuing outreach of the gospel to the nations. In Acts 8 the story of the conversion of the eunuch from Ethiopia is recounted and Wright sees significance in the fact that the eunuch reads from Isaiah, noting: 'Luke undoubtedly saw in this event a fulfilment of the promise of God to eunuchs and foreigners in Isaiah 56' (Wright, 2006, p. 516).

Continuing the pursuit of discovering multicultural encounters in Scripture, three further events stand out in Acts: Peter's meeting with Cornelius, the convening of the council in Jerusalem and the beginnings of the Philippian church.

The first is Peter's vision, recorded in Acts 10.9–23. Cornelius, a devout, God-fearing Roman centurion, has a vision revealing that he should send for Peter. Before those who are dispatched on the task reach Peter, he in turn has a vision in which it is revealed to him that he should not refuse food that is unclean. The significance of this unfolds when he goes to Cornelius's house and realizes God has released him to receive the hospitality of a Gentile. He says, 'I now realise how true it is that God does not show favouritism but accepts from every nation the one who fears him and does what is right' (Acts 10.34–35). Wright comments: 'A worldview shaped by a lifetime lived within the rules of Jewish food laws and the paradigm of segregation they symbolized was not easily set aside' (Wright, 2006, p. 515). The significance of this text in multicultural settings is evident. Here God's impartiality is affirmed and Peterson notes that the Greek word *dektos*, translated here as 'accepts', may better be translated 'welcomes' (Peterson, 2009, p. 335). In other words, 'God does not show favouritism but welcomes men from every nation.'

The second multicultural encounter occurs after Paul and Barnabas return to Jerusalem from their first missionary journey. A council has been convened in Jerusalem to come to a mind on whether circumcision is essential for the salvation of Gentiles. It is a disagreement between Jew and Gentile believers and is in danger of becoming a dispute between the church in Jerusalem and the church in Antioch (cf Acts 15.1, 24). Whereas the church in Jerusalem was predominantly made up of Jewish Christians, the church in Antioch was much more diverse (Acts

13.1). The fact that this issue had arisen demonstrates that Jews and Gentiles were now worshipping alongside each other, or at the very least were engaging with one another. However, some Jewish Christians were of the opinion that male Gentile converts should be circumcised, effectively becoming proselytes to Judaism, in order to belong to the church. The conclusion of the council was to affirm that circumcision was not required for Gentile believers. NT scholar Luke Johnson states that Luke

> uses the apostles' statements to shape a new definition of 'the people of God' as one based on messianic faith rather than on ethnic origin or ritual observance . . . He asserts unequivocally that the authentic people of God is one in which all nations can share as equals, and that since God has shown himself to be without discrimination, so must the church itself.
>
> (Johnson, 1992, p. 280)

Both of these events demonstrate the equality of Jews and Gentiles, something which will be explored further in relation to Paul's theology later in this chapter.

The third multicultural encounter worth noting in Acts is the founding of the Philippian church recounted in Acts 16.11–40. Paul's arrival in Philippi leads to a train of events that results in the conversion of three people: Lydia, a God-fearing Gentile woman from Asia Minor, likely to have been of substantial means (Peterson, 2009, p. 458); a local slave girl whose name we are not even given; and a Roman jailer. Johnson observes, 'It is possible to read this section of [Luke's] story as a snippet of the social history of the early empire . . . we see the multiform, pluralistic, and intensely vibrant life of the Mediterranean world of the first century' (Johnson, 1992, p. 302).

The context of this passage as described by Johnson reflects very well the multicultural contexts of twenty-first-century city life. The interaction of traditions and people of differing ethnic and cultural backgrounds provides fertile ground for authentic Christian communities to emerge.

Multicultural dimensions in the theology of the Apostle Paul

In Ephesians Paul writes that Christ's purpose was 'to create in himself one new humanity out of the two, thus making peace' (Ephesians 2.15). His concern as he is held under house arrest (Ephesians 3.1; 4.1; 6.20) is that the fledgling Christian Church should not descend into factions but in fact be united in Christ. In particular, that the believers will grasp the magnificent mystery of God that has now been revealed: that the Gentiles have now been drawn into the purposes of God in Christ (Ephesians 1.11, 13). In Ephesians 2 this theme is explored further as Paul lays out the situation of the Gentiles being 'excluded from citizenship in Israel and foreigners to the covenants of the promise' (Ephesians 2.12). He alludes to the Temple in Jerusalem, which had become a symbol of segregation by virtue of the fact that Gentiles could only occupy the outer court. The gateway to the inner courts displayed the sign that Gentiles could not pass on pain of death (Keener, 2003, p. 211). But Paul declares, 'For he himself is our peace, who has made the two groups one and has destroyed the barrier, the dividing wall of hostility' (Ephesians 2.14). Paul persists with the theme throughout the letter, stating, 'This mystery is that through the gospel the Gentiles are heirs together with Israel, members together of one body, and sharers together in the promise in Christ Jesus' (Ephesians 3.6).

Harold Hoehner, commenting on Ephesians 2.15, states, 'It is not that Gentiles become Jews as Gentile proselytes did in pre-NT times nor that Jews become Gentiles, but both become "one new person" or "one new humanity", a third entity' (Hoehner, 2002, pp. 378–9).[3] The maintenance of this tension between allowing ethnic distinctions to be upheld and at the same time stressing a unity in Christ among all believers is important in Paul's thought.

Drawing on this foundation in Ephesians, Scottish theologian Bruce Milne builds a case for developing a multicultural church:

Here is the great Ephesian image of the church. It is a new humanity, a community consisting of people remade . . . what is being
contemplated here is vastly more than a racial reconciliation . . .
the 'newness' is vastly wider and deeper, involving a fundamental
reconstitution of human relatedness, and hence inclusive of every
primary form of interpersonal alienation.

(Milne, 2007, pp. 21–2)

Daniel Boyarin, Jewish rather than Christian, and a self-confessed
critical but sympathetic reader of Paul (Boyarin, 1994, p. 1),
takes issue with Paul over what he sees as Paul's indifference
to ethnic and cultural elements that were important to Jews.
He focuses on Galatians 3.28 to argue that through baptism,
ethnic and cultural elements are negated, dissolved 'into a
single essence in which matters of cultural practice are irrelevant
and only faith in Christ is significant' (Boyarin, 1994, p. 9). Charles
Cousar challenges Boyarin's argument, asking, 'Do Paul's letters
reflect a concern, deliberate or unintended, for the suppression
of ethnic and cultural distinctiveness?' (Cousar, 1998, p. 49). In
response to this question, Cousar considers three texts: Galatians
3.26–29, 1 Corinthians 7.17–20 and Romans 9—11.

From chapter 3, Cousar argues that Galatians does not represent a polemic against Jews and hence an attempt to persuade
them to discard their cultural practices, but rather is written
to a Gentile readership who were being persuaded by some
Jewish Christians that they needed to become Jewish (Cousar,
1998, p. 50). This is reflected in Paul's comment on his disagreement with Peter in Galatians 2, which exposes a very real issue
within an emerging multicultural church. Peter, as was noted
above in the comment on Acts 10, has been led by God through
a vision to realize that God is impartial and that he himself
should not refrain from enjoying the hospitality offered by
Gentile believers. However, as Paul states, Peter has drawn back
from that position under pressure from certain Jewish Christians
who are seeking to persuade Gentile believers to be circumcised.

Paul recalls that he said to Peter, 'You are a Jew, yet you live like a Gentile and not like a Jew. How is it, then, that you force Gentiles to follow Jewish customs? We who are Jews by birth and not sinful Gentiles, know that a person is not justified by the works of the law, but by faith in Jesus Christ' (Galatians 2.14–15). Cousar observes,

> When Paul sets Christ over against circumcision in Galatians, he is not denigrating the outward ritual in favour of an inward, spiritual grace. Rather, the Messiah has come, and his coming entails at least two corollaries about the community: It is inclusive of Gentiles in line with the promise made to Abraham ... and its primary identity is not the Torah but the Messiah.
>
> (Cousar, 1998, p. 51)

The point is, then, that Jewish cultural elements remain significant for Jews, as indeed they had been significant for those who wished to assimilate among the Jews in the Old Testament period. Assimilation into Israel required compliance with the demands of the *torah*. But things have changed, and as assimilation into the new humanity is now through Christ, not the *torah*, then the requirements of the *torah* are no longer relevant to non-Jewish believers for them to belong. Paul then does not negate the cultural elements, but rebuffs those who seek to impose their own cultural traditions on others.

Paul's argument in 1 Corinthians 7.17–20 falls in the midst of a discussion regarding marriage and the situation of those married to unbelievers. It reveals a principle that resists the attempt to impose unnecessary regulation upon those who believe in Christ. Paul states, 'each person should live as a believer in whatever situation the Lord has assigned to them, just as God has called them', a statement that is repeated three times (vv. 17, 20, 24). This is not a moral 'free for all', for Paul himself says, 'Keeping God's commands is what counts' (1 Corinthians 7.19). Rather, as Cousar puts it, 'The call of God does not require a social or ethnic change on the part of the ones called. Jews are to remain Jews, and Gentiles are to remain Gentiles' (Cousar, 1998, p. 51). However, Cousar illustrates the complexity that arises in multicultural communities, pointing out in reference to 1 Corinthians 10.32: 'Paul seems more like a pastoral theologian urging a community of God's people to be sensitive to diversities that exist among them ... The health and integrity of the church, in the light of the message of the crucified Christ, becomes determinative' (Cousar, 1998, p. 52).

The third text that Cousar employs to reject Boyarin's accusation that Paul negates any ethnic particularity is Romans 9—11. He contends that Paul faced two problems. First, there were Gentile Christians who thought that they could live independently of the Jews. Second, there were Jews who had not recognized Jesus as Messiah (Cousar, 1998, pp. 52–3). Cousar remains uncommitted over how 'all Israel will be saved' but observes, 'For Paul, the inclusion of the Gentiles, while it created a dislocation for Judaism, was never meant to negate the commitments laid out in 9.4–6 or to signal a supersession of Jews by Christians or to require an ethnically homogenized community' (Cousar, 1998, p. 54). In his commentary on Galatians Cousar writes, 'the unity [Paul] declares is not one, in the first instance, in which ethnic, social, and sexual differences vanish, but one in which the barriers, the hostility, the chauvinism, and the sense of superiority and inferiority between respective categories are destroyed' (Cousar, 1982, p. 86).

In responding to Boyarin, Cousar cannot fully satisfy his demands in that Boyarin is seeking religious pluralism (affirmation of his Jewishness aside from Christianity). However, he goes some way to mitigate Boyarin's complaint by showing that Paul is supportive of ethnic pluralism, not seeking conformity but recognition and respect, in a context of diversity within the Christian community.

This significant aspect of Paul's theology appears in Colossians 3.11 where Paul says, 'Here there is no Gentile or Jew, circumcised or uncircumcised, barbarian, Scythian, slave or free, but

Christ is all, and is in all.' Hays points out that although the similarity between this verse and Galatians 3.28 is obvious, in Colossians Paul broadens the scope from just Jew and Gentile into the wider social, cultural and racial sphere. Hays goes on to describe the 'Barbarians' as those 'who did not speak Greek or did not live according to the Greco-Roman cultural norms' and the 'Scythians' as those who epitomized 'all the negative elements of the Barbarian' (Hays, 2003, p. 188). It is evident that Paul can conceive of no basis for ethnic or social prejudice.

The vision of a multicultural heaven in Revelation

This chapter and the previous one have sought to highlight the continuing theme throughout the Bible that God's will and purpose is to draw people from every nation to worship him. Here in Revelation, the ultimate climax of this persistent eschatological vision is revealed and articulated:

> After this I looked, and there before me was a great multitude that no one could count, from every nation, tribe, people and language, standing before the throne and before the Lamb. They were wearing white robes and were holding palm branches in their hands. And they cried out in a loud voice: 'Salvation belongs to our God, who sits on the throne, and to the Lamb.'
>
> (Revelation 7.9–10)

Different views on the interpretation of Revelation and the future realization of the kingdom of God abound, but for the purposes of the present discussion it is sufficient to observe that, in the vision given to the author of Revelation of what is to come, these verses envisage an enlarging of the circle of the redeemed. Biblical scholar Gregory K. Beale describes the purpose of Revelation as portraying 'an end-time new creation that has irrupted into the present old world through the death and resurrection of Christ and through the sending of the Spirit at Pentecost' (Beale, 1999, p. 175). He goes on to say that the application of these words for the Church is that they 'may continually be reminded of God's real, new world, which stands in opposition to the old, fallen system in which they presently live' (Beale, 1999, p. 175).

There is a progression in Revelation 7 from the 144,000 (reflecting the 12 tribes of Israel), to the multitude, and on to the culmination of all things, encompassing angels and all creation. The declaration in this vision that among the redeemed shall be a great number of people, too many to count, 'from every nation, tribe, people and language' is drawn on the one hand from the promise given to Abraham that his descendants shall be too many to count (Genesis 15.5; 22.17) and on the other from Daniel 7, which anticipates this event, foreseeing 'one like a son of man, coming with the clouds of heaven . . . He was given authority, glory and sovereign power; all nations and people of every language worshipped him' (Daniel 7.13–14).

The key aspect of this passage for us is the clear articulation that there are, and will be, among the redeemed in heaven people from every nation, tribe, people group and language.[4]

An emerging biblical framework for developing a multicultural church

Chapters 2 and 3 have sought to explore the multicultural dimensions of the Bible. In so doing we have attempted to read the Bible from a multicultural hermeneutical perspective and considered what insights and principles emerge from such reading. Out of this, four elements can be discerned which may serve to provide a biblical and theological framework for developing our thinking about multicultural churches.

First, an affirmation of diversity is prevalent throughout the Bible. This is evident in three ways. It has become clear that the Bible affirms diversity as God's will and purpose. Further to that, a study of the origins of Israel as a nation has demonstrated the ability and capacity of Israel to absorb differing ethnic and cultural streams. But another persistent theme has been the concern for God to bless 'all nations', which is ultimately reflected in the eschatological vision for the end of time.

Second, a tradition of assimilation (absorption into a particular culture), which is the predominant means by which people of other nations joined Israel in the Old Testament, and which requires circumcision and other rituals of adherence, develops into a tradition of integration (allowing cultural difference), becoming the predominant means (sociologically speaking) by which people of other nations join the Church in the New Testament. There is a clear shift from the rules that were prevalent in the Old Testament for those wishing to belong to the people of Israel, to Paul's pastoral negotiation of ethnic and cultural particularities in the New Testament Church.

Third, Jesus demonstrates a shift in attitude towards the other nations. If the Old Testament reflects an emphasis on what Routledge describes as a centripetal ('come and join us') approach to the other nations, then Jesus' actions and words encourage a greater emphasis on a centrifugal (sending out) approach to the other nations. This change in attitude also reflects a shift from acceptance of people of other ethnic and cultural backgrounds towards an active welcome of them.

Fourth, in the theology of Paul and the practice of the early Church, recognition and affirmation of a person's ethnic and cultural heritage prevail towards those who become Christians. Belonging to the new humanity does not necessitate a repudiation of a person's ethnicity. However, this is not an uncritical acceptance of any and all cultural behaviour and values; faithfulness to Christ and the health and integrity of the Church have become the controlling factors. But ethnic and cultural diversity is maintained and where differences lead to conflict, these are negotiated.

4

Multiculturalism in context

Given that the subject of how people of differing ethnic back-grounds relate to each other is not only important to those of us involved in multicultural churches but relevant for the nation as a whole, this chapter explores the main approaches to the matter debated in the public arena and considers their validity in the light of our biblical study in Chapters 2 and 3. We shall first discuss two approaches that are at opposite ends of the spectrum: the *assimilationist* and the *multiculturalist*. We shall then explore the approach of political philosopher Bhikhu Parekh, which attempts to reframe the way that we consider the issue and offers a more optimistic approach which will be shown to resonate more readily with the biblical view that has been set out. Finally we shall explore the issue of identity and consider its relevance to our discussion.

The assimilationist approach

Those who espouse assimilation insist that people of differing ethnic and cultural backgrounds who come to Britain should assimilate into British society, assuming British values, customs, language and worldview. Brian Barry, former Professor of Political Science at the London School of Economics, is typical of those who are opposed to pursuing multicultural policies in the political realm. He believes that liberalism depends upon ignoring a person's religion, ethnicity or culture. His view is that it is possible to discover universal principles and morals (such as democracy and women's rights) which supersede all cultural and religious particularity. Those holding similar views argue that such particularity can only be expressed in private and that the sole consideration for governments with regard to the spending of public resources should be in terms of need. The allocation of resources to religious, ethnic or cultural groups undermines this fundamental principle. Barry states his objection to multiculturalism bluntly: 'a politics of multiculturalism undermines a politics of redistribution' (Barry, 2001, p. 8).

Barry makes clear that his concern 'is with views that support the politicization of group identities, where the basis of the common identity is claimed to be cultural' (Barry, 2001, p. 5). He does not believe that it is sustainable to allow different ethnic and cultural groups to claim the right to live out their lives distinct from others, and states that to claim 'this is the way we do things' rejects a universally valid morality (Barry, 2001, p. 280). He rejects the idea that he is seeking, unfairly, to impose his values on others by stating that 'this is the way things ought to be done everywhere: we do things that way here not because it is part of our culture but because it is the right thing to do' (Barry, 2001, p. 284). This tension between universal morality and particularity is at the heart of the debate we are considering.

Barry outlines three claims which he reckons form the core of the argument for multiculturalism, and disputes each of them. First he contests the idea that you can defend a behavioural trait because it forms part of the culture of your ethnic group, stating that 'the fact that you (or your ancestors) have been doing something for a long time does nothing in itself to justify your continuing to do it' (Barry, 2001, p. 258). Second he rejects the notion that practices within cultures are immutable. He expresses concern that some are going so far as to revive the idea of biological fate in their determination to protect ethnic and cultural particularism, and that this denies the core liberal idea that 'there is a common emancipatory project equally available to the whole of humanity and equally valuable for all' (Barry, 2001, p. 261). He continues, 'precisely because human beings are virtually identical as they come from the hand of nature ... there is nothing straightforwardly absurd about the idea that there is a single best way for human beings to live, allowing whatever adjustments are necessary for different physical environments' (Barry, 2001, p. 262).

Third, Barry protests against the idea that cultures should be presumed or affirmed to be of equal value. He feels that this is a contradiction in itself, asking that if each culture is intrinsically different from others and must be affirmed from within its own frame of reference, then what basis is there for each to be compared to another and declared of equal worth? He feels that such an affirmation actually undermines the possibility of comparison and the useful emergence of any universal principles of significance.

As is clear from the previous chapters, assimilation was the way of belonging to Israel in the Old Testament. We can acknowledge that people of all ethnic groups were respected as equals, though their way of life was judged according to the *torah*. The way of life put forward in the *torah* was intended to be the way of life for all, and in that sense there was a legitimate claim for its superiority to those offered by the other nations.

Although Barry is British, his views have never reflected the British way of doing things. In the UK the view has almost always been taken that ethnic minorities are to be accommodated wherever possible. For example, Sikhs are exempted from wearing motorcycle crash helmets, and schools are allowed to serve halal food if there are significant numbers of Muslims attending. France has developed policies which lean much more towards the liberal assimilationist approach, for example enacting a law in 2010 that prohibited the wearing of a full-face covering (such as a burqa or niqab) in public places. It was argued that the wearing of the full veil in public was incompatible with the values of the French Republic, contrary both to the ideal of fraternity and to the minimum amount of civility that is necessary for social interaction. The law was challenged but in July 2014 the European Court of Human Rights upheld the ban, declaring that the preservation of a certain idea of living together was the legitimate aim of the French authorities.

Within the UK there have been attempts to promote 'Britishness' among migrants resident here, but there has been little agreement as to what that means, and so it seems unlikely that the more tolerant approach towards people of differing ethnic backgrounds will change very much in the foreseeable future.

The multiculturalist approach

Those who espouse multiculturalism in the political sphere see the role of government as the facilitator of those with differing ethnic and cultural backgrounds, and believe that it is a virtue to encourage self-expression as far as possible. Many supporters of multiculturalism take the view that society is enhanced and enriched by allowing a rich tapestry of culture and customs to be publicly manifest.

Will Kymlicka is a Canadian political scientist who has taken a keen interest in the rights of sub-state national groups. In 2007 he published *Multicultural Odysseys*, in which he argues for the need to promote liberal multiculturalism through international institutions. He traces the roots of multiculturalism through four United Nations (UN) declarations made between 1948 and 1992. Maintaining that ideas of racial or ethnic hierarchy persisted until the Second World War but that Hitler's policies finally discredited them (Kymlicka, 2007, p. 89), he claims that 'colonialism was premised on the assumption of a hierarchy of peoples' and that when it was accepted that European countries could not 'colonize' one another, there was no longer any rationale for them to colonize any other country, whether such a country was European or not.

The United Nations Declaration of Human Rights in 1948 was a repudiation of colonization in any form, made explicit in the 1960 UN General Assembly Resolution on decolonization.

In 1965 the UN Convention on the Elimination of All Forms of Racial Discrimination sought to link equality and racial discrimination in a way that buttressed the battle to overcome racial segregation in the United States and inspired similar struggles in other parts of the world. Then in 1992 the principle of multiculturalism came to the fore with the UN Declaration on the Rights of Persons Belonging to National or Ethnic, Religious and Linguistic Minorities.

It is worth remembering that Kymlicka has in mind three categories when he thinks of ethnic minorities: sub-state nations (for example Scotland and Wales in the UK), indigenous people groups (such as Aborigines in Australia), and immigrant groups (such as Pakistani people settled in the UK). He notes that support for multiculturalism is a policy option that is required as part of a commitment to human rights and equality rather than pursued out of any virtuous conviction: 'There's relatively little evidence that members of the dominant group have become "true believers" in multiculturalism in that sense' (Kymlicka, 2007, p. 120). He also observes that a retreat from multiculturalism with regard to immigration is occurring due to heightened security fears following the attacks of September 11, 2001 in the United States and the bombings in Madrid and London that followed (Kymlicka, 2007, p. 125). Indeed, support for a retreat from multiculturalism continues to grow in Europe as a result of instability in certain parts of the world, the rise of Islamist violence and the evidence that European-born Muslims are being radicalized and trained, not only to take part in terrorism abroad but also to launch terrorist attacks in Europe. In November 2015 attacks in Paris killed 130 people, raising questions as to how young people growing up in Europe can reject the European way of life. Clearly many young people of differing ethnic and cultural backgrounds have not integrated into European society. Anti-migration sentiment increases because of these attacks and Kymlicka concludes that 'many citizens are willing to accept multiculturalist policies when they are perceived as low risk, but oppose them when they are perceived as high risk' (Kymlicka, 2007, p. 127).

A further point made by Kymlicka is that his view of liberal multiculturalism must be distinguished from what he calls a traditionalist approach to multiculturalism. The traditionalist approach, as he defines it, requires that traditional ways of life must be preserved and protected, and even perpetuated, come what may:

> The liberal view of multiculturalism is inevitably, intentionally, and unapologetically transformational of people's cultural traditions. It demands both dominant and historically subordinated groups to engage in new practices, to enter new relationships, and to embrace new concepts and discourses, all of which profoundly transform people's identities and practices.
>
> (Kymlicka, 2007, p. 99)

At the heart of the dispute between Barry and Kymlicka is the issue of whether ethnic minorities need to assimilate in order to ensure they are brought into and benefit from the democratic process (e.g. learning the language, a willingness to vote), rather than being allowed to develop as independent enclaves within the nation. Political theorist Adam Tebble argues that for multiculturalism to thrive liberalism needs to prosper, actively seeking to integrate minorities into the mainstream, otherwise a multicultural society will degenerate into nationalism, with liberalism itself becoming marginalized (Tebble, 2006). The break-up of the former Yugoslavia serves to illustrate these fears. It is also notable that during the first decade of the second millennium in Britain, the rise of nationalism (leading to a surge of support for the Scottish National Party and the UK Independence Party) has been accompanied by increased hostility towards immigrants.

Parekh and the call to rethink multiculturalism

Lord Bhikhu Parekh, a political philosopher, comes to the debate from a different standpoint and offers a more optimistic approach. His argument is that liberalism itself emerges from Western culture, which one should not presume to be the best possible way of life for all: 'a [liberal] theory cannot provide an intellectually coherent and morally acceptable theoretical basis of multicultural society. We need to rise to a higher level of philosophical abstraction' (Parekh, 2000, p. 14). Elsewhere he writes, '[Multicultural societies] need to find ways of reconciling the legitimate demands of unity and diversity, of achieving political unity without cultural uniformity, and cultivating among its [sic] citizens both a common sense of belonging and a willingness to respect and cherish deep cultural differences' (Parekh, 1999).

Parekh proposes that this can only come about through dialogue, allowing a multicultural society to emerge and develop in a continuously evolving process. In doing so he rejects the monist approach which assumes a universal fixed morality, rooted in human nature, that is there to be discovered, and instead argues for something more fluid, that emerges and evolves through such encounters as happen every day in multicultural societies.

For Parekh there are two moral imperatives for pursuing dialogue between people of different ethnic and cultural backgrounds. The first is the greater insight into human morality that is thereby acquired. Parekh is concerned with 'what kind of life is worth living, what activities are worth pursuing, and what forms of human relations worth cultivating' (Parekh, 2000, p. 144). Morality is contextual (Parekh, 2000, pp. 132–4, 144), though Parekh recognizes that morals arrived at within particular contexts will contribute to a progressive approach that aspires to a universally valid morality:

Given the differences in their history, traditions and moral culture, it is both inevitable and desirable that different societies should differently interpret, prioritize and realize great moral values and integrate them with their own suitably revised thick and complex moral structures. This is the only way we can deepen our insights into the complexity and grandeur of human life and attain increasingly higher levels of moral universality.

(Parekh, 2000, p. 141)

The second moral imperative for dialogue is that it allows us to take a self-reflective view of ourselves within our own culture. For Parekh, our capacity to be self-reflective is an essential part of what it means to be human. It enables insight into our condition and the capacity to grow in our understanding and comprehension of who we are.

One of the significant benefits that Parekh identifies arising within a multicultural society is that it offers human beings greater freedom in understanding themselves and others than would otherwise be the case. It is liberating in that respect:

Unless human beings are able to step out of their culture, they remain imprisoned within it and tend to absolutize it, imagining it to be the only natural or self-evident way to understand and organize human life. And they cannot step out of their culture unless they have access to others. Although human beings lack an Archimidean [*sic*] standpoint or a 'view from nowhere', they do have mini-Archimidean [*sic*] standpoints in the form of other cultures that enable them to view their own from the outside, tease out its strengths and weaknesses, and deepen their self-consciousness. They are able to see the contingency of their culture and relate to it freely rather than as a fate or predicament.   (Parekh, 2000, p. 167)

There is much in what Parekh says here that makes sense when we think about the purpose and benefit of shaping and nurturing healthy multicultural congregations. Most of us, at some time, will have found inspiration from listening to a person talk from a different ethnic or cultural perspective. When people from differing ethnic backgrounds bring their insights to a passage of Scripture or a problem in church life, they often provide different perspectives and a greater understanding which can help strengthen a church. Similarly, the way one becomes conscious of one's own 'British' traits in speaking and acting in church life can help reveal just how much the British cultural way of doing things is assumed to be 'God's way'. Learning to put ourselves in the shoes of others, to see ourselves as they see us, can be enlightening. It is in community with others who are different from us that the ways we are different begin to show. But it is also the case that, as we discover more clearly our ethnic and cultural particularities, we are able to consider what is good and worthwhile and what values, customs and traditions may be better left behind.

In Ephesians 3.17–18 Paul writes, 'And I pray that you, being rooted and established in love, may have power, together with all the Lord's holy people, to grasp how wide and long and high and deep is the love of Christ.' There is a desire in Paul's prayer that every believer, of every ethnicity, should contribute to building a Christian cultural environment that is accessible to all and enables all to deepen their understanding of what it means to love and be loved by Christ. As we live and worship within a multicultural Church we grow more able to become the answer to Paul's prayer.

The impact of multicultural community on identity

Paul was very conscious of his own ethnic and cultural background. He described himself as born in Tarsus of Cilicia as a Jew, but was registered as a citizen of the Roman Empire. He was a descendant of the tribe of Benjamin, a Pharisee committed to upholding the law and had been mentored by Gamaliel (Acts 16.37; 22.3; Philippians 3.4–6). Paul's identity had also been affected by his conversion to become a follower of Jesus. He was now 'a servant of Christ Jesus, called to be an apostle and set apart for the gospel of God' (Romans 1.1). Not that he had discarded his previous identity; indeed he was still proud of who he was and where he had come from. But his identity had changed, developed and grown over time, as his life had changed. Avtar Brah, a sociologist, says, 'Identity is not an already given thing but rather it is a process. It is not something fixed that we carry around with ourselves like a piece of luggage. Rather it is constituted and changes with changing contexts' (Brah, 2007, p. 143).

Andy Jolley, who has served as vicar of a multicultural church in Birmingham, points to the importance of affirming individuals' cultural identity while at the same time building a shared identity:

> As well as creating space for each cultural group to express its own distinctive characteristics and to feel valued, it is also vital for a multicultural congregation to develop a shared story and identify what unites them ... Shared new experiences also offer a great opportunity to build a shared history or story that does not belong to a particular group or era.   (Jolley, 2015, p. 18)

A congregation in a relatively monocultural environment will have a fairly settled identity with a good deal in common between its members. In a multicultural environment people find they have much less in common with those around them and have to work much harder to develop a shared sense of identity and belonging together.

This is an important point to grasp, as there is a tendency to stereotype people very quickly in multicultural churches and begin to label them simply by their ethnicity and not much else: 'He is the Nigerian man', 'she is the Indian-looking lady' and so on. It is not unusual for people to be hesitant to talk to those of different ethnic backgrounds from themselves; they may struggle with their accent, or become confused as to who is who because to the inexperienced eye, people of a particular culture can look very similar. It is very easy to see a person just as we imagine him or her to be according to our stereotypical ideas. This is something we will discuss further in Chapter 5.

Parekh argues that identity is three-dimensional – there is our *personal* identity, our *social* identity and our *human* identity. Our personal identity refers to that part of ourselves which is unique to us, our bodies, our biographical details and our inner life and thoughts. It incorporates our beliefs and values, our character and how we seek to organize our lives. Our social identity refers to those aspects of our identity which embed us into social groups. It relates to who we are as members of families and ethnic or cultural groups; our religious affiliation, gender, employment, and membership of clubs and associations. Our social identity articulates how we relate to others and how others relate to us. Our human identity is what we share in common with all other human beings in the world and defines us as distinct from other species of animals. It is the identity that leads us to make demands of each other relating to such universal concerns as human rights and climate change. Parekh says, 'the three identities are inseparable and flow into each other' (Parekh, 2008, pp. 8–9).

Some academics consider that people have multiple identities. Parekh would resist this, claiming, as does Brah, that identities are not possessions we carry around. Rather we may present ourselves in different ways in different contexts and therefore have plural identities which put greater emphasis on the various aspects of our identity as we so choose. However, others also seek to label us in different ways and we will find it a struggle sometimes to identify ourselves the way we would like to be known. For example, when I am on holiday and someone asks me where I am from, I say London. I have lived in London longer than anywhere else and after all these years I feel more at home in London than I do elsewhere. Inevitably though, particularly if the person asking is British, they will detect a trace of a northern accent and go on to ask me, 'But you aren't a Londoner, are you?'

People from different ethnic backgrounds who join our congregations are not to become exotic exhibits but are to be respected and valued as our equals in Christ. They are not merely Jamaicans, Chinese or Nigerians, even though this is an incredibly important, relevant – and to begin with, the most obvious – part of who they are. They are also husbands, wives, sons and daughters; they are cleaners, administrators, architects, engineers, nurses, teachers, scientists and bank clerks; they love nature, watch films, like shopping, play sport; they are excited about birthdays and anniversaries, and are worried about what they hear on the news; they are Sunday school teachers, theologians, vicars, pastors, intercessors, flower-arrangers and so on.

Developing a healthy multicultural church depends in part on our ability not only to foster a sense of belonging together in Christ, but also to discover the things we share and identify with together, one to one throughout the congregation. That process of discovery takes us beyond the elements of our identity that distinguish us from each other and finds the common interests, experiences and passions, the ways that the different aspects of our identities can interweave as we share our values, explore how we can organize ourselves, become part of each other's social circles and stand with one another through thick and thin in our common identity as children of God.

From a sociological and philosophical point of view, Parekh offers a third way forward. Given that the assimilationist and multiculturalist ways of shaping communities have strengths and weaknesses and are both contested, Parekh invites us to consider a different way to approach the issue of integration. His view is that humanity can aspire to a better way of life, but that this will come about not by a reductionist or a multi-faceted approach but by a dialogical and evolutionary approach. Parekh's approach to the situation is to aspire to be the best we can through listening to and learning from one another. Rephrasing his statement quoted earlier, making it particular to a church context, sums up the task and challenge for every multicultural church:

> [Multicultural churches] need to find ways of reconciling the legitimate demands of unity and diversity, of achieving [spiritual] unity without cultural uniformity, and cultivating among [their members] both a common sense of belonging and a willingness to respect and cherish deep cultural differences.

Parekh offers an optimistic view of the multicultural community as one with great potential to develop in a way that enhances the growth not only of the individual but also of the community as a whole. There is no limit, in his view, to the heights we can reach as we engage and relate together. We shall turn, however, in the next chapter to consider what brings us down to earth with a bump – our prejudices.

5

Overcoming prejudice

Prejudice and stereotypes

Prejudice is a reality of everyday life, for everyone harbours prejudice to a greater or lesser extent. Prejudices take root for either of two reasons. One is ignorance: we believe that a certain group of people behave in a particular way because of mis-information we have accepted without knowing any better. The other is as a result of a bad experience: we have made the assumption that a whole group of people behave in a particular way because of a bad experience we have had with a few.

Consider this case study. A white British man in a multi-cultural church expressed his feeling that the reason other members of the congregation regularly came to church late was to do with their culture, because he believed that 'they are very laidback, time wise, in their country'. When asked which cultures this related to, he said he thought the people concerned were from the Caribbean. However, he also went on to say that he knew Jamaican people whom he described as 'punctual ones . . . one more punctual than the other', and later on in the conversation observed that he also had Jamaican neighbours who 'although they are Jamaican . . . are very different personalities to a lot of other Jamaican people I know'.

What we can see in the above example is how this man held a view that Jamaican people tended to be late for church. He also observed Jamaican people who weren't late for church. The question is, why did he believe that the reason certain people were late for church was to do with their ethnicity, even though the evidence was inconsistent? This is not unusual. If people allow a prejudice to form in their mind, they retain that prejudice even though the evidence doesn't bear it out. People stubbornly hold on to prejudices even when they discover evidence to the contrary. We call this process of labelling groups of people in oversimplified ways 'stereotyping'. The word stereotype comes from the field of printing, where it referred to a solid plate of an image or composed type which would be difficult to change once it had been created. When a person has formed a stereotype in his or her mind it becomes very difficult to break it.

What happens is that every time people come across evidence contrary to the stereotype, they treat that example as an exception to the rule. So, in the example above, the man in question saw his Jamaican friends as exceptions to his stereotypical view regarding Jamaicans in general, and he persisted with this stereotypical view even when he discovered his neighbours were among the exceptions to the rule. People generally resist the challenge to reassess their stereotypes even when they discover evidence contrary to the assumptions and generalizations they hold in their minds. Some people are more willing than others to break their stereotypes and learn from the evidence they see. Helping people increase their openness to breaking their stereotypes and giving up their prejudices is a necessary skill for leaders in multicultural environments.

Anxiety in multicultural environments

A factor which exacerbates the problem of prejudice is that when people become anxious their prejudices intensify as they look for scapegoats, others to blame for the situation they find themselves in. Research undertaken for the National Communities Forum (NCF) in the UK in July 2008 sought to consider the sources of resentment and perceptions of ethnic minorities among people resident in 'white' urban estates in England. Among the significant findings of this research was that some perceptions of unfair treatment experienced by the indigenous community were either exaggerated or simply untrue. One reflection on the research considered that where perceptions articulated as factual stories or rumours extended beyond what was actually true, these stories were to be understood as 'a coded way to signal that the speaker contests the frame within which all the unfairness is experienced by ethnic minorities. By doing this, the speaker's community is recast as the victim of discrimination' (Garner, 2009, p. 8). If we apply this to the local church, there are occasions when indigenous people begin to feel anxious about people of other ethnic backgrounds coming into their environment in increasing numbers. They may feel threatened, fearful of becoming a minority within their own church or of the changes to the status quo that will arise as a result. These fears inevitably lead them to begin to exaggerate issues and problems in church life and scapegoat others unfairly.

It is worth noting that the kind of anxiety that leads to scapegoating may not be as simple as the concern of white indigenous people about black or Asian immigrants. It may be the concern of white indigenous people about white eastern European immigrants, or anxiety arising from the presence of groups with other defining characteristics. A south Asian woman who had experienced prejudice herself when she arrived in the UK in the 1950s expressed in old age her feeling that the elderly people of the church (a group that was ethnically diverse) were being neglected as attention was given to newcomers who were themselves from diverse ethnic backgrounds. The task of recognizing and assuaging such anxiety is something every multicultural leader needs to be aware of.

An echo of this issue is found in Acts 6.1–6, where the apostles in the early Church faced complaints from Greek-speaking Jewish widows of neglect in the distribution of food compared to the apparent favour being shown towards Hebrew-speaking widows. In this instance a very practical solution was found by appointing a team familiar with the needs of the Greek-speaking widows to be responsible for ensuring those needs were met adequately and in a way equal to the care offered to the Hebrew-speaking widows. There is an element of contingency in the way the problem was resolved, as the initial outcome left two groups of people in the early Church being cared for by different teams based on their ethnicity. Such contingencies are sometimes needed in the short term until, as time goes by, the people concerned are better integrated and where necessary the structural life of the church or organization is reformed.

Allport's four conditions for overcoming prejudice

In the 1950s in the USA a significant debate raged as to the consequences of integration for a society that had grown used to segregation in factories, schools and public life. Many argued that to allow blacks and whites equal opportunities in the workplace, in schools and colleges and in public life would inevitably lead to greater trouble and hostility. They argued that if there are tensions between people then it is best to keep them apart.

Some saw things differently. One such person, Gordon Allport, a social psychologist, argued that integrating people of different ethnic backgrounds would in fact achieve the opposite, in other words a reduction of prejudice (Allport, 1979). His notion was essentially that prejudice arises out of ignorance and that when people grow in their knowledge and understanding of one another by working alongside one another, then prejudice diminishes. In his view, when people of different ethnic backgrounds worked together, studied together or campaigned together, then they would grow together.

Allport also stipulated four conditions that would help to ensure a positive outcome. First, he said, there must be 'equal status contact' between people. In other words there must be no discrimination towards anyone. Black or white people may rise to the highest positions in the company or have the opportunity to achieve the highest grades at school. Second, there must be a sense of working towards a common goal. If people are working together in a common cause, greater interdependence will inevitably be encouraged in order to achieve that goal. Third, there must be institutional support. For Allport, the company or school must be a multicultural environment and this status must be championed by the most senior authority figure in the organization. Fourth, there must be a perception of mutual benefit.

It is not difficult to see how relevant Allport's theory is to achieving harmonious relationships within a multicultural church. We can translate his four conditions to church life in this way:

1 There must be nothing to prevent an appropriately qualified person taking up any position within the church or Christian organization, regardless of that person's ethnicity.
2 People of all ethnic backgrounds must be encouraged to develop shared objectives and vision for the church or organization and to work together to achieve them.
3 Those in positions of authority must affirm publicly and regularly that the church is a multicultural environment and reflect that fact in the church's publicity.
4 The benefit of having people of differing ethnic backgrounds sharing church life together must be appreciated by all.

Each of these principles will now be considered in turn.

1 There must be nothing to prevent an appropriately qualified person taking up any position within the church or Christian organization, regardless of that person's ethnicity. The situation in which our churches find themselves in the early twenty-first century is very different from that which Allport was confronted with in the 1950s. In principle there is no reason why a person of any ethnic background cannot rise to be a committee member, a deacon, an elder, a lay reader, a vicar or pastor, a bishop even. Most, if not all, churches would declare that to be the case. However, in practice, things are not always how they seem. This is because of two factors which can, if not acknowledged, work against equality within the local church.

The first is that in a relatively small volunteer environment we often turn to people we know reasonably well when looking to recruit to positions of responsibility. We want to know enough about the person concerned to be sure of her character, her ability and her reliability. We may also want the person to be someone we can get along with comfortably. The problem here is that if the circle of those whom we know reasonably well happens to consist of people like ourselves, we perpetuate 'more of the same' in terms of the ethnic or cultural backgrounds of those assuming leadership responsibility. Unless we make an effort to increase our circle of friends to include those of different ethnic backgrounds from our own, we can very easily find ourselves only appointing to roles in church life people like ourselves. A further unfortunate consequence of this is that a perception takes hold in the minds of those of different ethnic backgrounds that only people of a certain type are ever appointed to positions of responsibility. They see who is appointed and how, and so they will hold back from putting themselves forward, believing, often rightly, that a person such as themselves will never be appointed.

The second factor which can prevent equality of opportunity within church life is the assumption of how a role or responsibility should be fulfilled. It is very easy to imagine that the next vicar, pastor, Sunday school teacher, church secretary or lay reader should fulfil the role in the same way as the current incumbent (and invariably in the same way as many before him or her). As a result, someone who may have held a position of considerable responsibility in his or her home country may well find that people do not see him or her as being able to fulfil a similar role in the UK.

One example is Theo. He was an asylum seeker from the Democratic Republic of Congo. To help him in the early days after he settled in the UK, the church he attended offered him some cleaning and caretaking work. This he did dutifully, and as time went on he established himself and his family, and found full-time paid work as an officer managing a local community centre. He continued cleaning and caretaking at the church. Ten years went by before it became known that Theo had been a leader of his church in Congo, had led the choir and fulfilled other leadership responsibilities.

It took a while before Theo could be encouraged to preach his first sermon in this church, because he was fearful that his English was not good enough. However, the church was going through a series on the fruits of the Holy Spirit at the time and he was asked to speak on 'patience'. He began his sermon in this way: 'The pastor has asked me to speak about patience. I did not want to speak about patience, I wanted to speak about peace. When I was five years old, my country gained independence and by the evening of that day we heard guns firing. I did not experience peace in my life until I stepped off the plane at Gatwick Airport as an asylum seeker. So I could say much about peace. But I have also seen that the reason we did not have peace in my country when we gained independence was because we did not have patience.'

Theo went on to speak about how we lack patience in our everyday lives and how this leads to a lack of peace in our lives. The congregation had to listen a little more carefully to catch every word he was saying, but nobody else in the church could have shared from the Bible on that theme in the same way because nobody else had lived out their Christian faith in that hostile environment.

There are many people from differing ethnic backgrounds whose gifts and abilities are under-used in the Church because people become used to seeing others in particular ways and have formed stereotypes that are difficult to break. Building relationships with people of different ethnic backgrounds from our own is essential to increase our awareness of a person's experience and potential to serve.

2 People of all ethnic backgrounds must be encouraged to develop shared objectives and vision for the church or organization and to work together to achieve them. This element is about working out a vision for the church community in practice, week by week. The fundamental purpose of every church is to draw people together to worship God and live out the gospel. It is that which draws people to belong to the Church and in that sense those people have a shared objective, whether spoken or unspoken. However, the most successful way to integrate this vision throughout church life and for it to be owned by all the members of the congregation is by making a commitment that whenever and wherever possible, every team or committee will be multicultural. Encouraging people from different ethnic backgrounds to come together for a specific purpose gives them the best opportunity to build cross-cultural friendships and develop better understanding, mutual appreciation and respect. When vacancies arise in existing teams, we have the chance to intentionally look for those whose backgrounds are different from those who are already serving and encourage them to become involved. This will often require asking people directly rather than making such a request publicly or through a newsletter.

The question that is often posed is whether taking such an approach constitutes tokenism. By tokenism it is meant that people are being appointed to roles in the church because of their ethnic background. There is often, quite rightly, a resistance to tokenism, or to acting in a way that seems to be nothing more than politically correct. However, we need to be careful that, in resisting tokenism and the pull to act in a politically correct manner, we avoid failing to act intentionally to empower people from different ethnic backgrounds who would help us strengthen our churches. We would be guilty of tokenism if people were being appointed to positions of responsibility on the basis of their ethnicity alone. However that is not what I want to encourage here. The principle of appointing people who are appropriately qualified remains important, but we should also recognize that although such people may be present in our churches, they are often overlooked because of their ethnic background. Intentional action is required to correct that error, and to ensure that such people have an equal opportunity to take up responsibility in church life.

Another way to make sure this happens is to ask, are there no members of the ethnic minorities in our church who could do the flowers, steward on a Sunday, make coffee, lead a service or preach a sermon? This underscores the belief that churches are stronger and better integrated if people of different ethnic backgrounds are encouraged to work together to achieve the vision of the church.

Allport observed that people from differing ethnic backgrounds were much more likely to grow in their understanding and respect for one another if they worked together on a task, rather than if they were asked to talk about themselves in an artificially created environment. Away days and racial justice training are popular among various denominations, and they have an important place, but the most effective way to develop an integrated environment is by asking a diverse group of people to accomplish a task together.

3 Those in positions of authority must affirm publicly and regularly that the church is a multicultural environment and reflect that fact in the church's publicity. If you were to walk into your church building when it is empty, read your church's newsletter or look at its website, what clues would there be that your church welcomes people of every ethnic background and is in fact already a congregation born of many nations? This is particularly important in contexts where the congregation is diverse but the leadership or those in upfront roles are predominantly of a single ethnic background. In such contexts, people of other ethnic backgrounds are effectively being called to be pioneers in that environment by stepping out and carrying responsibility. This can be intimidating for such people as they look around for others who have been a steward, a church officer, a committee member or performed another such role for some time and are comfortable in that environment, and find that there are few or none like themselves. They may feel the added pressure of being the first black or Asian person to carry out that role. As a result they may feel themselves to be under the spotlight. Others may unfairly judge their ethnic group as a whole by how well the individual fulfils his or her role or responsibility. People of the individual's own ethnic group may well be watching how well he or she fares in the new role and whether she will be accepted by the wider community. It is important in such situations to have a public voice affirming and encouraging diversity and the value of diversity. Such a voice, expressed by those in positions of influence and reinforced in the church's publicity, will over time shape the expectations of the majority and give support and encouragement to those ethnic pioneers in church life.

I once visited a church where in the congregation of about 400 I was one of only two white people present. I visited the church a few years later and was one of a dozen. I also noticed that there was a white person in the music group, and that white and black people were featured together on an advertising banner. What I observed was the intentional message that white people were welcomed and could take on significant roles in this predominantly West African church. Even for a confident person like myself, these visible signals in prominent places helped me to feel that there was a place in this church for someone like me.

4 The benefit of having people of differing ethnic backgrounds sharing church life together must be appreciated by all. Allport was convinced, even in 1950s America, that if people of different ethnic backgrounds learned, worked and played together, over time they would grow in mutual appreciation and eventually discover that the quality of life for them all was enhanced. However, if the perception remains that integrating people of different ethnic backgrounds is a necessary evil, then there will inevitably be a negative drag on any initiatives to move forward in this area. It is important therefore to help people discover the benefits to be enjoyed in a multicultural church.

When integration takes place sensitively and appropriately, then benefits may be found in three areas. First, it can result in increased participation by the congregation. One continual challenge for church leaders is the recruitment of volunteers to help out. Serving in church life is often a sign that a person feels at home and belongs to the church, and is part of his or her own spiritual growth. Often in churches whose congregations include significant ethnic minorities, such people are under-represented in serving and leading roles. There may be practical reasons why this is so: for example it may be that those from ethnic minorities work longer hours, while migrants are less likely than long-term residents to have wider family available to help with childcare. Both factors can make it more difficult for members of ethnic minorities to participate fully in church life. It is likely, however, that with the right approach many of them will be keen to be more involved and the benefit to the church will be tangible.

Second, it can lead to an improvement of the spiritual life of the church. It is well documented that the Church in the Western world has suffered from declining attendances and the pervasive influence of secularism, both of which often undermine the confidence of Christians. Those who come to our churches from parts of the world where the Church is more vibrant inevitably bring some of that vibrancy and confidence in their faith to our own congregations. It is fair to assume that in places such as London the waves of immigration between the 1950s and the present day have saved many churches from closure as Christian immigrants have replaced in the pews indigenous British people who have drifted from church over this period.

Third, it can lead to an increase in the individual's awareness of and confidence in living and working in an ethnically diverse environment. A multicultural church can be a place where people grow in understanding, learning about different cultures, following differing accents, discovering diverse customs and practices. It can be a place where we can ask questions and travel the world through the people we meet.

One woman said, '[When] I went to university I lived in a predominantly Asian area which was like a slum. I used to think that Asian people were dirty, and that is a terrible thing to say, so it's been good to chat to people from an Asian background at church and get to know people and actually challenge those preconceived ideas.'

A doctor from Sudan said, 'If I had any problem with approaching English people, [then] through the church it is so normal to me now. I can talk to anybody on the street, and the same to any African, Nigerian or Asian or Indian, so it just makes it so easy for me to approach any person.'

Pursued sensitively, the benefits of being a part of a multicultural church begin to show, and people benefit from personal growth as a result.

Overcoming prejudice in the early Church

Earlier in this chapter we noted the situation in Acts 6.1–6, where the apostles were faced with an issue with an ethnic element as the Greek-speaking widows were treated differently from the Hebrew-speaking widows in the distribution of food. In the light of Allport's insights we can now see how the way the apostles handled the situation demonstrates the validity of his four conditions:

1 Equal opportunity for all. The apostles were keen for the continuing mission of the Church not to be held back by inequality in the distribution of food to the widows. They needed to show that there was to be no discrimination within the Church, so they acknowledged the problem, called a meeting and implemented a structural change to put things right.

2 Building multicultural teams with a shared vision. At first glance it seems the team appointed were not multicultural and so Allport's second test was failed! However, it is noticeable that the team had some relation to the widows, being of Greek-Jewish origin, and included Nicolas 'from Antioch, a convert to Judaism'. These newly empowered team members were appointed from among the local church community. They were selected not just because they had language skills or were from that sector of the community, but because they were people who had a love for God and a desire to see the church grow. This was not tokenism – merely appointing them because they spoke the same language as the widows – but because they could do the job and do it well. This is reflected in the successful resolution of the issue, and evident in that the good news continued to spread and many more became believers (Acts 6.7).

3 Leadership in declaring the church to be multicultural. It is evident here that the apostles did not shirk their responsibilities in this regard or pass it on to others to resolve. They both recognized and affirmed the importance of the matter publicly by taking the lead in resolving it. They called a meeting of all the believers, decided what needed to be done and then passed the matter back to those involved locally to implement their plan. Their involvement was a signal to all that everyone in the Church mattered and needed to be included and cared for.

4 Experiencing the benefit. In Acts 6.5 it says that everyone was pleased with the idea put forward by the apostles. It was a win–win situation: the Greek-speaking widows were cared for, more of their community were involved in the serving ministry of the Church, the apostles were freed from the problem to concentrate on the mission of the Church, and the Church continued to move forward and grow.

Overcoming prejudices and building a healthy multicultural environment is not just about keeping everyone happy, but is about the ability of the members of a church to fulfil their potential in Christ. Allport helps us identify the problem of prejudice but also offers us the tools to overcome such prejudice and create a more inclusive environment and a mobilized Church.

Conclusion to Part 1

In Part 1 of this book I have attempted to outline three foundations for developing an inclusive church environment. The first of these has been to establish from Scripture that the purpose and plan of God was to call a multicultural people to love him, serve him, and make known the gospel to all the peoples of the earth. The second was to show how in the context of the secular world there is, from Bhikhu Parekh, a philosophical argument that a multicultural community offers the best kind of community in which to live. The third has been to draw from the research of social psychologist Gordon Allport in order to understand how prejudice grows and to consider practical ways that it can be reduced and overcome, so enabling us to be a more inclusive church.

In Part 2 we will build on these foundations by applying the above insights to four areas of church life: worship, pastoral care, leadership and mission.

Part 2

WORKING IT OUT
IN PRACTICE

6

Approaches to worship

———•◦•———

Worship space is a country without borders, a place where citizens are not people who hold documents but people who live in each community. *(Carvalhaes, 2011)*

The encouragement for people to participate is essential to the development of an inclusive multicultural environment. This is particularly true in the area of public worship, which is often the first encounter people have with a church and will offer the earliest impression of how inclusive a particular church has become. Christopher Ellis, author and editor of several books on worship, writes: 'There is something very specific about leading worship. You are called to lead this community of persons in this place on this day in the worship of God. Worship should be contextual, sensitive to the particularities of the people and the situation' (Ellis, 2009, p. 25).

If the vision is there, then intentional steps can be taken to ensure that the diversity of contributions develops. Of course, such a development is not without its difficulties; in some denominations it will be limited by the constraints of the liturgy, while there may be those in the congregation who are not happy to see their customary style and conduct of worship change.

Laurene B. Bowers, an American minister in the United Church of Christ, recognizes that there is a tension here which can only be resolved if worshippers look beyond their own personal needs to create space for the needs of others in the overall texture of church life and worship. She writes, 'What is important to those who worship in multicultural church is that the diversity of worshipers transforms the worship, often in unexpected ways, and that wonder and mystery take priority over likes and dislikes with respect to worship styles and musical preferences' (Bowers, 2006, p. 119). Bowers touches on something significant here, recognizing that the diversity of worshippers results in a transformation of the worship. But this in itself necessitates a shift in attitude on the part of the worshipper, from seeking a form which suits one's personal style and preference, and to which one has become accustomed, towards allowing space for the worship to reflect the diversity of those present. Mark DeYmaz, founding pastor of a network of multi-ethnic churches in Arkansas, USA, states that 'it is in worship that leaders must begin to promote a spirit of inclusion' and that members of the congregation must recognize that 'they are part of something much bigger than themselves' (DeYmaz, 2007, pp. 109–10).

It is self-evident that for this transition to take place the indigenous host community must sacrifice something of what is familiar to them to create the space for those from other ethnic backgrounds to express themselves. Eric Law, a Chinese-American Episcopal priest, highlights the sacrifice necessary in what he describes as the 'cycle of Gospel living in a multi-cultural community' (Law, 1993, pp. 73–4). He argues that those who hold power in a community must be prepared to give away such power to enable those who have none to be empowered to participate fully in the community. Subsequently, as those who then gain power participate more fully, they in turn must be prepared to give it away to others in a continual dynamic of mutual invitation to participate. Law relates this process to Matthew 19.30, 'but many who are first will be last, and many who are last will be first', saying that 'the movement from being powerful to powerless and then from powerless to powerful is the dynamic of the Gospel' (Law, 1993, p. 61).

There is a clear resonance here with the issue of worship in multicultural churches. In order for those of differing ethnic backgrounds to participate fully, those who are occupying the space must be prepared to step back and allow others to come forward. This empowering of people to participate enables them not just to lead from the front in a way that is in the tradition or custom of the church or the host community, but to allow for something of what is distinctive in their cultural worldview to become evident as they lead. Law recognizes that this process may necessitate endurance and faithfulness on the part of those who are presently excluded, enabling them to struggle patiently until the moment of invitation comes, but when it comes, it offers an opportunity for both the dominant and the minority cultures to enter a cycle of gospel living in which all are empowered by the death and resurrection of Christ. The extent to which those in power are motivated to make sacrifices, and the congregation as a whole is willing to make space for those from differing ethnic backgrounds, is the extent to which a church can progress from acknowledging and respecting such people to valuing and cherishing their presence and contribution in church life. It is to come to appreciate that they have something to offer which, if it remains hidden, will leave everyone impoverished in some way.

Developing inclusion in worship

The first way that inclusion can be nurtured is simply by encouraging members of the congregation from differing ethnic backgrounds to take a turn in contributing at regular services in ways that require little by way of training and do not entail formal appointment, such as reading Scripture or leading prayers or a song (whether for all to sing or as a solo). They may also be invited to participate in the variety of background roles available, such as helping to welcome people, make refreshments and so on. Many multicultural churches, of all denominations and none, find this the obvious starting place from which to increase the diversity of those participating in public worship.

The next step is often to invite members of the congregation to participate using their own language or mother tongue, whether with translation provided or not. Creative ways can be used to allow people to use their mother tongue without the need for constant translation, for instance by giving the congregation the English translation on a handout sheet or using multi-media screens to display translations while the language is being spoken.

It may be asked why this is a useful thing to do. If English is the commonly spoken language, why encourage people to speak in their mother tongue? To what extent will this feel akin to a gimmick, to entertainment maybe? On the other hand, to what extent does such activity reflect an understanding and working out of the gospel and contribute to the healthy development of a church? Three reasons why it is good to encourage people to share in worship in their mother tongue are offered here.

First, it can be liberating and affirming for a person to speak, worship and pray in a mother tongue when otherwise, if speaking in English, one may have to translate as one speaks and may thus lack fluency. For example, Jieun was a young South Korean woman who spent a gap year serving on the team of a local church. She willingly prayed openly at team prayers but it was hard for her to express herself in English. When invited to pray in her mother tongue her prayers flowed and, even though the other members of the team didn't understand the language, they found her prayers inspirational and uplifting, and understood their flow. Afterwards she would sometimes give a summary of her prayer. In fact, it is surprising just how much can be understood if one is listening carefully.

In smaller groups where people know one another well and there is a high level of trust, offering the freedom to speak in a mother tongue can work effectively. In a wider context, it will be helpful to provide translation in some way. Allowing participation in a member's mother tongue helps to create a welcoming and affirming atmosphere in the church and the opportunity is often deeply appreciated by those who normally worship in a language not their own. Even those present whose own language or culture is not expressed will see that their church is a place where everyone is welcome for who they are, and with the languages they speak.

A second reason why it is good to encourage people to participate in this way is that it widens the perspective of all who worship in a particular church. Every church is part of the 'one holy catholic and apostolic Church' and there are people all around the world, people we think of as our brothers and sisters in Christ, who are worshipping God in their own language. God hears the prayers of his people in the languages of the world, and for a local congregation to hear them at first hand broadens their perspective of the nature of the Church. For one Christmas carol service I chose a few verses from each of the traditional readings and had them read in a different language by someone in the congregation. We had angels speaking in Spanish, Tamil, Yoruba, French and Polish! Concerned not to allow the readings to become tedious by having the whole passage read in a different language and at the same time not to allow them to distract from the theme and message of the service, I arranged for the English to appear on the screen while the verses in foreign languages were spoken. The participants valued the opportunity to speak in their mother tongue, while those listening appreciated both hearing the languages and how this reflected the diversity of our congregation.

The third reason why it is good to encourage people to participate in their mother tongue is that it reminds us of the multilingual context of the Bible. This may seem an obvious point, but in Britain most people have grown up speaking and, with most television and radio being broadcast in English, hearing only one language. Even when British people travel they find they can negotiate their way around in English in most parts of the world. For those brought up freely reading English translations of the Bible it can be hard to think of people in the Bible speaking any other language. Yet many people in the world live in multilingual environments, often speaking languages imposed by former colonial powers, regional languages and local dialects. It may be helpful therefore, from a global theological perspective, to shift congregations in some small way towards a multilingual environment. It may help people to think of themselves as part of a worldwide church. It may help to subtly reduce a sense of superiority and allow people to recognize that English is only one of the languages of heaven. The point here is not to undermine English as the usual, dominant language of communication in an English-speaking environment, but equally not to dismiss too quickly the notion of appreciating the diversity of languages known and spoken in a multicultural church.

Contributing songs either in a mother tongue or traditional hymns and songs with a different rhythm or style is a useful way to encourage participation. Even in liturgical churches, songs and hymns are not limited by the constraints of the liturgy and therefore allow for variety of cultural expression. However, caution is needed for two reasons.

First, it is important not to allow a false sense of achievement to develop in the area of inclusion in worship simply because people of a different ethnic background have been allowed to lead a song or two in church. This can only be the beginning, not the end of the inclusion process. This process, at least in the area of music, must in time enable fusion in all aspects of music in the church, allowing different rhythms and styles to make their mark.

Second, when people bring songs from 'home', the children of those sharing these songs, who may have grown up in the UK, may well roll their eyes and speak of their 'parents' songs', and may not necessarily want to be associated with them. It needs to be recognized that such songs can become anachronistic, failing to reflect the tastes and preferences of the following generation. This can be a problem for expatriates everywhere, existing as they often do, so to speak, in a cultural bubble. By way of example, consider the 'British Polo Day' held in Beijing, China. The order of events includes a champagne reception, afternoon tea and the Royal Salute. There is nothing wrong with wanting to celebrate one's culture, but a day such as this only reflects a small aspect, and a rather traditional class-bound one at that, of British cultural life today. There is a similar danger for expatriate congregations in the UK if they continue to worship in the same style, using the same songs and the same version of the Bible as when the congregation was first established. There are expatriate congregations which risk becoming unable to attract new members because their worship style has not developed and probably bears little resemblance to the contemporary worship styles of their home countries. These congregations have a role to play in providing pastorally for those who appreciate them, but they may struggle to be viable self-sustaining congregations in the future.

A similar problem arises if, by encouraging participation in this way within one of the mainstream denominational churches, one is simply providing space for traditional renditions of songs and music from those communities rather than reflecting contemporary expressions of worship within their cultural and ethnic style. Again, the fusion of styles in the overall pattern of a church's music is the way forward both for mainstream denominations and for expatriate congregations.

A third step towards developing inclusion in worship is to consider the origin and source of the materials used. One can begin with the visual art and posters on noticeboards around the church premises and assess to what extent they promote a multicultural environment. Consideration can be given to who has produced these materials and what prejudices may be evident. The ethnicities of the writers of any songs that are being sung may also be examined, as may the style and language used. Developing inclusion in these areas will not happen quickly, but needs thought, experimentation, creativity and persistence. Worship workshops, in which the writing of hymns, songs, prayers and poems within multicultural groups can be encouraged, may help to produce new material to serve the church in this way.

Intercessions

Another important area of public worship which can be developed is the intercessions. People of differing ethnic backgrounds can bring to these insight and first-hand knowledge and experience. A person who has contact with family or friends in a country facing conflict, or where Christians are persecuted, or where there has been a tsunami or flood, earthquake or disease, can enrich the intercessory prayer life of a congregation; that person's first-hand experience of the situation can help the congregation connect to issues that feature (or otherwise) in the media. When the Ebola virus was spreading rapidly in a number of West African countries during 2014–15, a member of our congregation visiting from Sierra Leone was unable to return home. She was able to speak with first-hand knowledge of the impact of the disease on her family and her church, and of those known to her who had fallen sick or died. The combination of information and the emotional impact upon her enabled the congregation to share the suffering of those affected and offer prayer and practical help with a much deeper sense of connection.

Government elections taking place in the countries from which members of the congregation originate can often create a sense of heightened concern over what the future will bring for those countries. Potential changes in government may have much more far-reaching consequences for those countries than are usually experienced in the West. Being aware, listening to the hopes and fears of those involved, and praying that such elections may have an equitable outcome shows interest and support, enables pastoral care, and helps to develop a greater awareness of the political situation in such places.

Towards a multicultural liturgy

One area in which it will be more challenging to develop a multi-cultural approach to worship is inclusion in the liturgy. Practice varies from denomination to denomination, but variations and translations of liturgies have been developed in different parts of the world in an attempt to relate more sensitively to each national or linguistic context. The question here is whether there is scope for further development.

Delbert Sandiford, former Executive Officer for Minority Ethnic Anglican Concerns in the diocese of Southwark, notes, 'This is an area where experimentation needs to be encouraged and resources developed. Creating multicultural liturgy is not part of the standard curriculum of theological colleges, and clergy may not feel confident in pioneering such an initiative on their own' (Sandiford, 2010, p. 22). Ian Tarrant, an Anglican cleric who has experience in the Democratic Republic of Congo, considers some of the reasons why people may want to stretch the existing boundaries of the liturgy in such contexts. He lists four reasons: first, to be more accessible to new people; second, to communicate timeless truths through new imagery and symbolism; third, to explore new ideas; and fourth, to savour new experiences (Tarrant, 2012, p. 6). Although Tarrant writes with new expressions of church in mind, it is not diffi-cult to see the resonance for those seeking to develop liturgy within multicultural contexts. He outlines areas where there is room for creative interaction with the liturgy to tailor it to suit better the local context and notes that there is plenty of scope for flexibility within the overall structure. Churches working within an authorized liturgical context will need to be mindful of being innovative in the parts where it is permitted to do so, whereas those in 'free church' contexts will find themselves with greater liberty.

Jonny Baker, a leading advocate of alternative worship, pushes the boundaries further:

> Curators in the early days of alternative worship discovered contextual, feminist, liberation and black theologies that were seemingly beyond the [liturgy], at least of their own tradition or starting point. Listening to voices from other contexts exposes where the [liturgy] is read from, through whose eyes, with the idea that it is simply a perspective rather than the final word. This opened up the possibility of doing contextual theology and reading with postmodern eyes.   (Baker, 2010, pp. 16–17)

There is clearly room for further thought and study with regard to this area of worship, and such thought may well be informed in the future by insights gleaned from those researching global approaches to theology. Nevertheless, beyond the bounds of the authorized forms, there is the opportunity for creativity and innovation.

Although many churches encourage people from differing ethnic backgrounds to participate in the liturgy in various ways, there is little experimentation – other than translation – with the liturgy itself. Tarrant suggests, among other things, the possibility of setting parts of the liturgy in diverse musical styles to bring creativity, encourage a different perspective and make it more memorable (Tarrant, 2012, p. 25).

A multicultural liturgy is not seeking to be cross-cultural; in other words, it is not seeking simply to translate language and idioms so that they are more easily understood in another language and culture. Rather it is seeking to be more relevant and accessible within a multicultural environment. It cannot be all things to all people, but it can exemplify an approach to life and worship that affirms the benefit of diversity for all. There are aspects of the liturgy which reflect very well a

multicultural vision of the Church. Take for example this extract
from a prayer for the season of Epiphany:

> Blessed are you Sovereign God, king of the nations,
> to you be praise and glory for ever.
> From the rising of the sun to its setting,
> your name is proclaimed in all the world.
>
> (The Archbishops' Council, 2015)

Parts of the liturgy such as this are drawn from Scripture,
much of which, as we saw in Chapters 2 and 3, clearly promotes
a multicultural worldview. So how can liturgy, and its use,
be developed further, not only to carry a greater resonance
in multicultural churches but also to aid the development
of multicultural communities? Here are three ways that the
development of a distinctly multicultural liturgy may begin:

**1 To include in the liturgy, where possible, brief parts of it
translated into a number of different languages.** For example,
take the acclamation,

> Christ has died, Christ is risen, Christ will come again!

It would not be a difficult thing for this acclamation to be said,
in a multicultural church, in three languages that are spoken
in the congregation, for example:

> Christ has died, Christ is risen, Christ will come again
> Christ est mort, Christ est ressuscité, Christ reviendra
> (French)
> Kristi ti kú, Kristi ti jinde, Kristi má padá wā (Yoruban)

If this were done often enough, everyone would quickly learn
this Gospel acclamation in the different languages used, and
over time other languages could be interchanged with those.
This would be interesting for the indigenous members of the
congregation and affirming for those whose language was being
included, while those with other mother tongues would be

encouraged to know that their language too could find a space. It is common practice in my own church to conclude a communion service with the Grace:

> May the grace of the Lord Jesus Christ,
> and the love of God,
> and the fellowship of the Holy Spirit
> be with you all.   (2 Corinthians 13.14)

Over a period of time I took the opportunity to invite someone to come and say the Grace in his or her own language before we all said it together in English. The woman who spoke it in the Maori language is often remembered because of how beautiful the words sounded on the ear, and how they stirred the heart. Anglicans may feel that in a multicultural church this would be in the spirit of Article 24, which says, 'It is a thing plainly repugnant to the Word of God, and the custom of the Primitive Church, to have public Prayer in the Church or to minister the Sacraments in a tongue not understanded of the people.'

2 To consider how theological and contextual perspectives from across the world may be incorporated more purposefully in the liturgies we use. In Chapter 2 it was noted that many in the world carry a sense of shame before God and their family for their sins rather than a sense of individual guilt. This could be reflected in a form of confession in this way:

> Lord God, you forgive us our sins and remove our shame.
> Lord, have mercy / Kyrie eleison

> You heal us by your Spirit.
> Christ, have mercy / Christe eleison

> You raise us to new life in your Son.
> Lord, have mercy / Kyrie eleison

Another example would be the assumption that we in the West are in a strong position to help those who are weak without recognizing that the 'we' includes many who were once far away geographically and are now here. For example, during the recent refugee crisis when many fled the conflict in Syria, many denominations offered a prayer for use by their congregations. Often those prayers lacked any acknowledgement that there were already a significant number of people in their churches who had been, or were, refugees seeking asylum. So consider this extract from such a prayer:

> We thank you for opening the hearts of many
> to those who are fleeing for their lives.
> Help us now to open our arms in welcome
> and reach out our hands in support.[1]

Being mindful of those members of our congregations who have been or are refugees could lead to the prayer being rephrased like this:

> We thank you for opening the hearts of many
> to those who are fleeing for their lives.
> Some of us were once refugees
> and you heard our cry
> and answered our prayer
> and brought us to a safe place.
> Help us together to open our arms in welcome
> and reach out our hands in support of others.

An even more inclusive way could be to invite refugees (or those who have been refugees) to contribute to such a prayer as this with their own idioms, their own turn of phrase, or in their own language.

3 To consider the accessibility of the liturgy to those for whom English is not their first language. There are of course contemporary versions of the liturgy and these will be particularly helpful to people whose understanding of English is limited. There is also much to be gained by listening to the way people from differing ethnic backgrounds speak. For example, an extempore prayer for healing by a British person may use language such as 'Lord we pray that Joyce may know your healing touch in her life.' An Afro-Caribbean member of the congregation might pray, 'Father God we pray for Joyce; we pray that you would heal her from the top of her head to the tip of her toes.' Those from other ethnic backgrounds often exhibit greater confidence in prayer and directness in their language and it may be appropriate to incorporate such ways of speaking into the style of the prayers and liturgical sentences we use. We can draw on all traditions available to us to develop and shape new prayers and sentences. I always find it strangely engaging to listen to my old Nigerian friend begin his prayers, 'Good evening Father, good evening Son, good evening Holy Spirit'; this form of words conjures up in my heart and mind the immanence of God much more vividly than the rather circumspect approach which often characterizes the British way of speaking.

Movement is also an aspect of worship that is worth considering. Many cultures are considerably more physically expressive in their worship than the British. Developing a permissive atmosphere in worship that allows expression of praise, thanksgiving or confession through movement, dance or appropriate gestures may prove to be appreciated over time. Shacoya was a young member of our church from the Turks and Caicos Islands and had a love for expressive dance, usually to black gospel music. I encouraged her to dance in church one day, which elicited from some of the white British people the response 'It was OK' and from some of our black Caribbean members 'Pastor, the dance was wonderful'.

It would be unfair to conclude from this anecdote that all white people will merely tolerate expressive dance, while black people will delight in it. Black gospel music rarely found a place in our worship services at the time and it was not often that a black person would be seen at the front. Such factors may have heightened the experience of Shacoya's expressive dance among the black Caribbean members. It was also the case that some of the white British members took the view that solos and dances were for the theatre and not for church services, immediately prejudicing their mind and attitude towards something that was offered as worship to God. I share this example to help us consider how we can use the resources available to us in our churches, which may not be to the taste of all, to enhance the depth and relevance of our worship service for others, and allow us to appreciate what each of us can bring. There will be an element of experimentation that has the potential to go wrong as well as to be a blessing, but this is part of the risk of the journey of becoming a multicultural church.

Preaching

Another area of worship that varies across cultures is the style of preaching. In Britain the dominant forms are expository (expounding the scriptural text verse by verse in a lecture-style approach), narrative (revealing the message through problem, plot and resolution) or simply an informative talk based on the Bible. However, Afro-Caribbean congregations have brought new approaches to preaching. Mark Sturge, formerly General Director of the African and Caribbean Evangelical Alliance, describes the experience:

> The preacher is at the heart of the worship in [black Pentecostal churches]. The onus is on the preacher to let the Holy Spirit 'fall' ... This creates the worshipping preacher, who cannot rely merely on expository preaching or exegeting a text since he or she might then be considered dead, dry or to lack the anointing. Consequently, sermons are punctuated with 'call and response' interaction to ensure the audience is 'feeling' the preacher: calls like 'Can I have a witness?', 'Is anyone there?', 'Hello?', 'Are you with me?', or 'Say praise the Lord somebody!' are responded to with shouts of 'Amen!', 'Hallelujah!', 'Preach it!', or 'Bless him, Lord!'   (Sturge, 2005, pp. 123–4)

Black American academic and preacher Henry H. Mitchell expounds what he calls the powerful art of black preaching. He writes, 'we bring to God our very best and ask God to take both preacher and congregation and make between them a sermon experience in which the Word and will are communicated with power' (Mitchell, 1990, p. 124).

He draws out some characteristics of black preaching, six of which are described here:

1 An emphasis on what God is saying rather than the personal opinion of the preacher (Mitchell, 1990, p. 56).
2 A sense of continuity with the generations that have gone before. Mitchell notes, in the African-American community the Bible is often quoted with the opening 'My mother (or father or grandfather or grandmother) always told me ...' (Mitchell, 1990, p. 58). This is because historically within these communities biblical teaching was passed from generation to generation orally, in a similar way to how the Hebrew oral tradition speaks of 'the God of Abraham, Isaac and Jacob'.
3 Imaginative elaboration that seeks to 'breathe life into both the story and the truth it teaches'. Mitchell writes that 'more vivid (but no less valid) details ... help the hearer to be caught up in the experience being narrated and, as a result, to understand better and to be moved to change' (Mitchell, 1990, p. 63).
4 Finding oneself in the Bible. Mitchell observes:

> Another imaginative aspect of Black preaching is the choice of illustrations – gripping modern parallels to the biblical text. In the process of making the point clear, the Black experience is lifted up and celebrated, identity is enhanced, and the hearer enters vicariously into the story, making it his or her own personal story.   (Mitchell, 1990, p. 66)

5 Dialogue between preacher and congregation. We have already noted Sturge's observations but Mitchell goes further. He differentiates authentic responses from those that are merely

habitual or manipulative; what he calls 'an Amen from the heart' from the non-thinking response where the member of the congregation is reacting without hearing. He writes:

> Real dialogue ... occurs characteristically in response to the preacher's mention of something that is vital in the life experience of the respondent – something with which the hearer identifies deeply. The congregants are able to respond because they are at ease. They are interested in what the preacher is saying, because they are crucially involved in the issues considered, and deeply interested in the Bible, from which the sermon comes. (Mitchell, 1990, p. 102)

6 Empowerment. Mitchell observes that Martin Luther King's 'I have a dream' address 'was in fact a sermon, which drew dialogue from thousands and moved the Civil Rights cause forward by giant steps on many fronts' (Mitchell, 1990, p. 108).

Another approach to black preaching is proposed by theologian and author Anthony Reddie. He approaches the task through the prism of Black Theology, which he defines as 'the attempt to rethink the meaning of God as revealed in Jesus, who is the Christ, in light of the historical and contemporary struggles and suffering of Black peoples, for the ultimate purpose of liberation' (Reddie, 2009, p. 77). Reddie is concerned for preachers to engage with the political realities of oppression in the world and to see in Scripture the resources to address these issues in their preaching. He uses the example of the parable of the Talents (Matthew 25.14–30) to show how a different interpretation of Scripture is possible. He sees the master as oppressive and exploitative (v. 26) and the third servant, who simply returns the master's investment, as the one who refuses to be used by his master in that way. Unlike the first two servants, who do what is required to protect themselves from punishment, the third, though armed with his excuse, will simply no longer allow himself to be used to earn money for his master. Reddie argues that we should not understand this parable in terms of using the gifts God has given (a popular interpretation); rather, he says, the point of the parable is that the kingdom of heaven is not like this exploitative situation at all. Moreover, the parable that follows is equally important to the context of the story, so its conclusion is that when the son of man comes in his glory (Matthew 25.31) this oppressive and exploitative master will suffer his comeuppance and the servants will truly receive their reward.

As with music in the church, so also with preaching there is scope for variety, for the appreciation of different styles with, as Parekh puts it, 'a willingness to respect and cherish deep cultural differences' (Parekh, 1999). The leader of a multi-cultural church has many wells from which to draw and the potential to develop a richness of ministry that takes inspiration from many sources.

Churches hosting expatriate congregations

We cannot consider the question of Sunday worship within multicultural churches without discussing a closely related area, which is that many churches in multicultural areas host one or more expatriate congregations, either at the same time or at different times of day. The identity of these separate congregations is often, though not exclusively, based on language; so, for example, there are Tamil-speaking congregations, French-speaking Congolese congregations, Chinese-speaking congregations and Polish-speaking congregations meeting throughout the UK.

These congregations vary in their relationship with the host congregation. Some merely rent the space, some have a friendly supportive relationship at a leadership level, some have members which attend both the host congregation and the expatriate congregation; some share services, either monthly or more occasionally, and some have a more formal structural relationship. It is clearly important to maintain a good relationship between the host congregation and the expatriate congregation, and many share occasional worship services to express their unity in Christ. Following the thinking of Allport, which we discussed in Chapter 5, it is worth considering how such disparate congregations may enter together into a task to develop their friendship, improve their mutual understanding and by so doing, increase the quality of their shared worship experience. An occasional collaborative worship service, however carefully constructed, may feel somewhat contrived. A thanksgiving service after a season working together to provide a temporary night shelter for local homeless people, for example, may well feel more authentic, having arisen out of a genuine partnership in the gospel. Similarly a shared mission, or a retreat or weekend away, may provide an atmosphere within which friendships grow and prejudices and language difficulties are overcome. Out of this, perhaps, worship will flow more freely.

7

Navigating the pastoral challenges

In my first year as a full-time minister, a young Ghanaian couple in the church were looking forward to the birth of their first child. One Sunday morning the proud father came to church and announced to me that the child had been born. I duly visited the family at home during the week, and in passing they said that they would be bringing the new baby to church for the first time the following Sunday.

When Sunday came they arrived at church all dressed up for the occasion and accompanied by family and friends. It dawned on me that they were expecting an infant dedication (as is our practice in the Baptist churches). Their indication to me that they would be bringing the baby to church for the first time was, in their minds, their way of saying they would like their baby blessed, as would have been the practice at their church in Ghana. I was so used to people bringing their newborn babies to church for weeks, if not months, before finally arranging a time for an infant dedication that it never crossed my mind that their expectation was for an impromptu ceremony as soon as mother and baby were ready to come.

I would love to say that I celebrated with them and included the appropriate liturgy and prayer of blessing for the child, improvising regardless of what was planned for the service that day. Looking back now, even if I hadn't been able to alter what was planned I could have followed the service with something special for them. But in fact, as a young, inexperienced minister, I froze, mumbled how our way of doing these things is to prepare in advance, and as a result hastily rearranged the blessing for the following week.

It pains me to share this story, as I still feel my discomfort every time I think of it. I wonder what that family must have thought as they went home disappointed after looking forward to a family celebration. Yes, it was a misunderstanding on both our parts, but one from which I could have recovered better and muddled my way through to cover the embarrassment we were all feeling. I sometimes look back at this incident as my baptism of fire into the unpredictable world of multicultural church and all the pastoral implications that emanate from it. I realized very early on that I would make many errors of judgement as a minister, because I wouldn't always understand what was being said and what the expectations were of me in a given situation. I also realized that I would need to learn to be flexible and adaptable, because no amount of ministerial training can prepare you for every cross-cultural encounter which comes your way.

A culture of discomfort

Kathleen Garces-Foley has coined the term 'a culture of discomfort' to describe the atmosphere within a multicultural church. Reflecting on her research within an Asian-American church in Los Angeles, USA, she observes that churches seeking to be multicultural will only succeed if they can live within an ongoing culture of discomfort. She writes,

> Discomfort is a subtler problem than tension or conflict, but it is a greater burden on church communities than it first sounds. In the sociological literature, it is widely thought that the primary reason people join a church is to satisfy basic needs of meaning and belonging. The discomfort of the multiethnic church makes it more difficult for these needs to be met.
>
> (Garces-Foley, 2007, p. 121)

Garces-Foley recognizes that there is a cost involved in pursuing diversity. People cannot have everything their own way but must give ground to allow others to express themselves too. When a majority culture exists in a church, then those in the majority must continually attempt to be sensitive to those in the minority and make adjustments to help them feel a part of the church. Those in the minority bear the weight of feeling they are on the margins of church life, seen as different, stereotyped. Michael Jagessar, Secretary of Racial Justice and Multicultural Ministry for the United Reformed Church, concurs, saying that we need to form an intercultural habit 'grounded on mutuality in giving and sharing: where we are all in need; where we all must be inconvenienced for the sake of the other and the gospel' (Jagessar, 2011).

The congregation's expectations of the church leader

It is not possible to know everything about the customs of all of the different people that make up a multicultural church. And even if it were possible to do so, customs differ not only between people of the same ethnic group but also over time. Some will prefer to follow their traditional customs as precisely as if they were still living in their own country. Others will more readily fuse their own customs with local practices and be willing to change and adapt. It is important to take time to listen, ask questions and be flexible in order to accommodate such cultural preferences.

A new person walking into the church may have different expectations from others coming to the church and this creates the potential for misunderstanding. Another man from Ghana asked, after he had been coming for a few weeks, why I hadn't visited him. It was his expectation that if I cared about him I would have visited his home and received hospitality from him. I figured that if I made a home visit to a British person who had recently begun attending church he would probably think I was being too pushy. Some people from certain Asian backgrounds tend to see the church leader as their personal family 'priest', invited to bless whatever family occasion may be happening at the time, whereas others may likely think that their church leader would be the last person to invite to their party! Attending some occasions as the minister will find me ushered to pride of place, a seat at the top table, whereas at other times I will be left at the back of the queue and probably find myself helping to sweep up afterwards. People of many cultures will offer food when a person visits their home; it would be unthinkable for them not to, even if the visit is unannounced. As a result there have been many days spent visiting members of the congregation when I have had lunch and snacks throughout the afternoon, arriving home at dinner time barely able to eat anything more. On the other hand, while one person offering tea as you arrive thinks they are demonstrating exemplary hospitality, to a person of another culture it can show that they are hoping that you won't stay too long!

The pastoral care ministry within a multicultural church will provide many surprises, more than I can recount. New ways that people do things (and the significance behind them) are likely to be discovered all the time. It becomes a journey of diplomacy and tact to negotiate your way through the potential misunderstandings, which it often seems are just waiting to trip you up.

Births, marriages and deaths

When a new baby arrives it is customary for a church leader to visit the family and join in celebrating their new arrival. Some cultures will have a naming ceremony and some will choose to have male children circumcised (facilities are usually provided by the NHS in multicultural areas to enable this to happen safely). A British church leader may or may not be asked to get involved in cultural practices surrounding the birth but some families will ask, and will hope that the church leader is ready to be involved. Improvisation is sometimes required to create a liturgy that fits the occasion while being biblically and theologically appropriate. I have already shared the story of my own misunderstanding regarding one family's expectation of an infant dedication, and although baptisms or infant dedications are something mainstream churches are conversant with, one has to be watchful of variations. Talking through what will happen and asking if anything should be included that would make the occasion feel more personal and culturally appropriate may prove helpful. Often the participation of a relative or friend reading a scripture, offering a prayer or singing a song from their country of origin can enhance the occasion, for the benefit not only of the new parents but of all who are present.

Marriages too provide a variety of patterns and need careful preparation. In some countries and cultures there are three parts to a wedding: the traditional betrothal, a civil ceremony (where the certificate is issued) and a blessing in church. It is not unusual for couples who have had a traditional betrothal and maybe a civil ceremony in their home country to then request a wedding blessing in the UK. Some may want simply to be married following the usual conventions of the denomination or church network here in the UK while adding some flourishes that reflect their heritage. In certain cultures it is expected that the wider family will be involved in agreeing on a marriage, how it may take place and whether payment of dowry is part of the arrangements. To some extent this is no different from a traditional British marriage, especially between a younger couple, who will discuss with their parents the best way to facilitate the marriage, who should be invited and who will pay for different elements of it. Church leaders may often be unaware of what has taken place among the families involved in the wedding preparations, though sometimes tensions surface and guidance is sought. Differences in expectation between the older and younger generations, those raised in traditional ways and those raised in the West, may generate conflict, and compromises will inevitably have to be made. There is the potential for conflict of traditional cultural practices with what may seem Christian practice, but given that the annals of British missionary history have many stories to tell of the imposition of Western culture, it is wise to find friends who understand these cultural practices to help one think them through carefully.

There will be times when you may want to gently confront certain practices which seem oppressive or feel inappropriate, but consultation will stand you in good stead to understand how to do so in the best possible way. For example, one couple came to me for advice having become exasperated with their families, who were unable to settle certain issues regarding the dowry and in the process had delayed the wedding several times. We resolved the matter by setting another date and informing their families that the couple would be married on that day, come what may. The issues were soon resolved.

It is impossible to anticipate every situation, and with increasing numbers of marriages taking place between couples of differing ethnic backgrounds, careful preparation is essential both to listen and take the time to be clear what the participants are asking for, and to consider how to accommodate their cultural preferences. Being sensitive to cultural issues that are causing stress in the preparations is important too, as a thoughtful church leader can help solve problems in ways that the couple may not have thought of.

Funerals are another area of ministry that varies between cultures. My experience has been mainly in British and Afro-Caribbean communities, but whatever the diversity in your church the principles of remaining flexible, adaptable and ready to improvise will serve you well. Generally people of other ethnic backgrounds appreciate that you may not understand all that is happening, but finding friends who do will help you greatly. Building good relationships with other church leaders in the local community who are from similar ethnic backgrounds to those you serve will provide a good place to turn to for insight and advice in negotiating cultural expectations at such times.

In Afro-Caribbean cultures the usual expectation is that family and friends will visit the home of the bereaved as soon as they hear of the death, whereas in others, including British culture, the bereaved may often want to be left alone. In multicultural churches embarrassment can be caused when people from Afro-Caribbean cultures turn up unannounced at a bereaved English person's home to support the person in his or her grief. On the other hand, when someone among the Afro-Caribbean community dies their relatives may wonder why none of the English people have come to support them in their grief. It is traditional in some Caribbean communities to have a gathering on the ninth night following a person's death. There is likely to be music and food; sometimes, if the church leader is invited, the evening may begin with a short ceremony including songs, prayer and Bible reading. These are often helpful expressions of support to the bereaved, and are to be encouraged.

When it comes to the ceremony itself, members of some cultures will want the coffin or casket to be opened in the church for a final viewing before the deceased's body is taken for burial. As the body is buried they will want family members to help fill in the grave as the mourners sing traditional songs. These songs are not likely to be among those used regularly in church, so clarifying who will be leading the singing and if words will be available is the kind of preparation which will help to avoid any embarrassment on the day. On these occasions no one leaves until the grave has been back-filled and the flowers arranged on top. Such occasions are often well attended, uplifting and accompanied by a variety of tributes, spoken and sung.

This can be a challenge for a church leader who has previously been involved only in British-style funerals. One funeral I attended, that of a Jamaican man who lived in a predominantly white area, was delayed because the groundsmen at the cemetery had gone elsewhere to dig another grave, assuming that the mourners would leave the grave for them to fill when they returned. The family were unable to back-fill the grave themselves because the clay soil was so heavy, but the wife of the deceased insisted on staying for over an hour, waiting for the workmen to return and fill the grave before she would leave to go on to the reception. This illustrates how important cultural practices can be, and how therefore it is necessary to ensure nothing is assumed and that everyone involved in the funeral is aware of what is expected.

However, even as one becomes familiar with the traditional customs of a particular culture, practices change over time. When I began full-time ministry in the 1990s, it was rare for someone of Afro-Caribbean background to request cremation. Now it is much more common. In the past, it would have been unthinkable for many to have the burial or cremation first and a thanksgiving or memorial service in church afterwards, but now it happens. Customs and traditions don't stand still but change over time, sometimes through choice and sometimes as a result of practical considerations.

Improvisation is often required: for example, when someone has died in another country and his or her relatives in the UK are unable to travel to the funeral. I once sat with a family as the funeral service for their mother took place in their home country of Pakistan. We sang the same hymns together, prayed and read appropriate scriptures before sharing in a meal to honour their loved one. It can seem strange at first to British church leaders when people ask to photograph or film a funeral in much the same way as a wedding, yet this has become more frequent as the desire to share the occasion with relatives across the world has grown. I have conducted funerals and weddings with family members using the church wireless network to transmit the service live to relatives elsewhere in the world via phone or tablet, enabling them to participate in some small way.

The need to develop an adaptable and flexible approach is emphasized by Delbert Sandiford:

> It becomes difficult to hold all this together by seeking to impose
> a particular set of cultural values. Yet with diverse values
> ministry can be scary. Some flexibility, willingness to go with
> the flow, capacity to learn on the hoof, and ability to 'tune
> the bandwidth' as you face scary situations seems like a good
> starting point. Leadership in such situations calls for some
> different skills from those normally applied to a culturally
> homogenous organization.   (Sandiford, 2010, p. 24)

Just as significant at these times of life as the practical arrangements is how to offer spiritual support. Essentially, the joy
surrounding a new birth, the stress of arranging a marriage,
and the grief at the loss of a loved one are similar the world
over, but how such joy, stress or grief is expressed can vary
greatly. You may hesitate to become too closely involved when
you are unfamiliar with a family's cultural practices, but willingness to see past the particular cultural ways of marking these
transitions in life and to bring faith, hope and love to people
is important. We must not feel that, because we are not sure
how people from a particular culture go about things, we
cannot, as church leaders, step into the situation and do what
we have been trained to do. Ministry offered with sincerity and
grace is always appreciated.

I have found that developing my own ways of doing things
that transcend culture can be useful. After discussing with a
family the arrangements for a funeral I will ask them all to stand
and join hands while I give thanks for their loved one and pray
for those who remain. Whatever their cultural background, or
whether they are strong believers or nominal in their faith, it's
an approach that all seem to appreciate, giving comfort and
encouraging togetherness within a family that is mourning. It
may be that it works for me because it suits my personality and
style, but I think that the church leader has an important role
to play in bringing spiritual support, guidance and blessing in
the preparation of funerals. The best approach is on the one
hand to be sensitive to each culture, while on the other doing

what is true to your own personal style – being yourself and ministering from a sincere and compassionate heart.

I have occasionally noticed that a member of a bereaved family has some church leadership experience, is a lay reader or particularly able to pray, read a scripture or bring a word of encouragement. That person may nevertheless be deferential towards me as a church leader, or uncertain whether I will be willing to allow him or her to participate alongside me. I have found it helpful, with the consent of the immediate family, to invite such gifted people among friends and relatives to share in some of the informal times of prayer in the preparation of a funeral or at the rehearsal for a wedding, bringing a word of encouragement at gatherings following a death, or in appropriate ways in the service itself.

It is worth reiterating at this point that misunderstandings will occur, mistakes will be made, and the potential to offend inadvertently is always there. However, people are usually understanding and forgiving, and we should not fear seeking to do our best – even though we may at times feel we don't really know what's going on! Again, taking the time to ask questions, clarifying what is expected, and drawing on trusted friends who understand the culture will always help to ease any discomfort we may experience.

A multicultural pastoral care team

We noted in Chapter 5, as part of our consideration of the outcomes of Allport's research, that it enhances the integration of a multicultural church if as many teams in the church as possible include members from differing ethnic backgrounds. This is particularly so with the pastoral care team. The church will be better able to respond sensitively to the needs of members of differing ethnic and cultural backgrounds if there are people in the team who understand the context of the need. The apostles in Acts 6 resolved the need among the widows by appointing people who identified with them ethnically and culturally (Jolley, 2015, p. 6). Awareness of the dynamics of the church with regard to pastoral care is important if one is to be able to provide the best possible care while at the same time facilitating better integration and improving mutual care across the congregation. This is not to say that in order to offer appropriate pastoral care a church needs to appoint to the team a person from every ethnic background represented in the congregation. But it is to recognize that sensitivity to intercultural issues requires the input of those who have experience crossing cultural boundaries and can understand how others may feel. There are often resonances between cultures which carry similar characteristics – for example the obligations to the family or wider community, the approach to hospitality, the customs around a death in the family. This means that bringing some diversity to a team will enable the team to become more sensitive across all cultures. It helps the individual members of the team to increase their capacity to think cross-culturally, to be more aware of what they may not know, and to approach situations with greater wisdom.

The need may also arise to provide support with issues often associated with migrants, such as immigration, poverty, accommodation and education. Many charities, often church based, have a wealth of expertise in these areas and may have food and household items available to support those in need. Working in collaboration with others and developing a good network of contacts will help the pastoral team to serve those in your church well.

Dealing with racism

In Chapter 5 we explored prejudice and considered how stereo-typing and looking for scapegoats can result in racist attitudes. Raleigh Washington and Glen Kehrein (black and white respec-tively) are two pastors who founded a church in Chicago with the deliberate intention that it should be multicultural.

They write, 'One of the struggles in cross-cultural ministry is the degree to which race figures into every issue. At one extreme are people who think race doesn't figure in at all – it's just a personality conflict, or a disagreement over direction. At the other end are people who see everything as a racial conflict.' They go on to say,

> When a black person is willing to be honest and really express what he or she feels, the white person is often shocked at the intensity of feeling about racism. But the reality is that racial discrimination has scarred or touched every single black person to one degree or another; it's alive today, like a burn that has never completely healed, so the 'skin' is very sensitive. The black person may not want to risk being honest, fearing another burn.
> (Washington and Kehrein, 1993, pp. 165–6)

Prejudice and racism does not only occur between people of different skin colour but may be expressed between any ethnic groups, and can have deep roots and complex expressions: for example, between English and Irish, Romanian and Romanian Roma, West Africans and people from the Caribbean. Nevertheless, the legacy of the particular history of the European slave trade continues to manifest itself regularly in relations between white and black people. Many black people who have experienced racism in church life will say nothing about it. Others will make sure that everyone knows when an incident occurs. The difficulty for the leader of a multicultural church when an accusation of racism occurs is threefold: hearing the two sides of the story and knowing that they will be very different; understanding the impact of the racist incident on the person who has suffered an injustice; and bringing reconciliation, forgiveness and healing.

When I began my first full-time ministry, two black families had recently left the church because they believed it, or individuals in it, to be racist. Although I hadn't been at the church at the time, I was the one seeking to bring healing, forgiveness and unity as we went forward together. It was important for me to take the time to listen carefully to what people were saying without making any initial judgement. I realized, too, that I needed to take what happened very seriously, and I looked to trusted black colleagues to help me understand why the families who had left were so angry. We then acknowledged as a church that we needed to improve our intercultural understanding, so we invited our denomination's racial justice officer to lead us through a series of studies to help us talk and listen to one another better.

It proved a difficult but helpful exercise, not least because we found at the end of it that we were able to talk about racial issues without becoming defensive or angry and this paved the way for better relationships to flourish as time went on. It was reassuring for all that we had attempted to take the issue seriously and do something about it rather than brush it under the carpet. The two families never returned to the church – sometimes the sense of rejection and hurt can be too deep for people to easily find the will to forgive and reconcile – and it is fair to say that often when people move on, they prefer not to go back. It was, however, necessary for the church to work through, understand and move forward from a difficult conflict in their journey together.

Reconciliation

Croatian theologian Miroslav Volf writes out of personal experience of conflict within the former republic of Yugoslavia. Committed to encouraging reconciliation, he draws on the relatedness of the Trinity to develop the metaphor of embrace as a way of conceiving how strangers can overcome the separation that arises from oppression, prejudice and fear (Volf, 1996, pp. 109–10). Volf writes,

> When the Trinity turns toward the world, the Son and the Spirit become ... the two arms of God by which humanity was made and taken into God's embrace ... That same love ... seeks to

make space 'in God' for humanity ... Humanity is, however, not just the other of God, but the beloved other who has become an enemy ... We, the others – we, the enemies – are embraced by the divine persons who love us with the same love with which they love each other and therefore make space for us within their own eternal embrace. (Volf, 1996, pp. 128–9)

Volf describes the metaphorical embrace as taking place in four steps. The first step is the opening of one's arms towards the other. This he describes as a sign of desire, of having created space in oneself for the other, and a gesture of invitation. He recognizes that in this act there is risk involved. Will the invitation be accepted or rejected?

The second step is what he describes as the waiting. Crucially Volf recognizes that the other cannot be forced to embrace; to do so would be to violate the other. He writes, 'Before [the embrace] can proceed, it must wait for desire to arise in the other and for the arms of the other to open' (Volf, 1996, p. 142). He notes that the power of waiting with arms open can move the other to reciprocate but though a boundary has been opened, it cannot be breached: 'Waiting is a sign that, although embrace may have a one-sidedness in its origin ... it can never reach its goal without reciprocity' (Volf, 1996, p. 143).

The third step is the closing of the arms where each enters the space of the other and can feel the presence of the other in the self. 'In an embrace a host is a guest and a guest is a host' (Volf, 1996, p. 143). Volf recognizes that this can be an unequal embrace, but it must never turn into a 'bear-hug' where one smothers the other.

The fourth step is the opening of the arms again. Volf insists that this release is necessary as a recognition of difference. In the embrace the two do not become one. Their identities do not merge as one, though they will inevitably be changed, even transformed, by the embrace. In releasing the embrace, the arms are open again, in a renewed posture of invitation (Volf, 1996, p. 145).

This metaphor of embrace, rooted in a relational understanding of the Trinity, offers a theological approach to reconciliation within and among diversity. It is not that unity becomes the same as uniformity (a concern of Parekh's, as we saw in Chapter 4), and neither is unity something that is static, a state of being. Polish sociologist Zygmunt Bauman writes that unity is something emergent, 'put together through negotiation and reconciliation, not the denial, stifling or smothering out of differences' (Bauman, 2000, p. 178).

The application of Volf's metaphor is relevant in two ways. It reflects the Church's embrace of the people of differing ethnic backgrounds who come to it. The welcome offered by the Church is not tacit but active and seeking an embrace. The person entering the church is hesitant, wondering what kind of welcome is being offered, what kind of community is this church, whether there is a space for 'someone like me'. He or she may have experienced prejudice previously and may experience contradictory feelings: will this welcome prove sincere or will I be opening myself to further hurt and rejection? I helped an elderly Jamaican man pack up his flat when he decided to return home to spend his final years. He was a quiet man, but as we worked I asked him what his experience had been of the churches he visited when he first came to the UK. He replied, 'Me and my friends, we went to the first church and they didn't give us books, they thought we couldn't read. We went to the second church and they asked us to sit at the back. We went to the third church and we were asked not to go too often because it was putting off some of the regulars. I didn't go back to church after that, I worked on Sundays, until I retired, some thirty or so years later, then I went back.' There are many stories like this one, stories of people who expected to find a welcome, find friends, find a spiritual home, but instead found themselves unwelcome, and were left to make their own way. Such experiences can make people hesitant to enter again, and risk rejection once more.

When the offer of the embrace is reciprocated, then the church and the one entering begin to share the same space, affecting each other as they do so, at one and the same time expressing love and yet making themselves vulnerable to each other. The visitor has found a spiritual home. But in the embrace and subsequent release there has been not only recognition of their unity in Christ, but also respect of their ethnic and cultural distinctions; the two have not become one. The diversity between people is recognized within the unity and an acknowledgement is made that there remain spaces between them which still need to be explored, gaps which need to be bridged.

The second way that Volf's metaphor is relevant is between individuals within the congregation. People can be part of a congregation, even one of say 50 people, for years without ever speaking to one another, particularly if they are from differing ethnic backgrounds. When an offer of embrace is made, an opportunity to spend time together, to work on a task together or to play together, there may be an initial reluctance. This is often the case with those from minority ethnic backgrounds who find themselves within a majority white congregation. However, one white woman who belonged to a mixed congregation described to me her feelings when she and her husband were invited to a house group meeting with people who were mainly of ethnic backgrounds different from their own. She said, 'There can sometimes be uncertainty about how to do things, what's the way of doing things, not to offend anybody.' She continued,

> It was the first time that we've ever really been in a minority. I did feel, perhaps, a little bit pushed back maybe, and there are some points when a mother tongue is used between groups, and that kind of isolates you a little bit because you don't really know what's going on, because you don't understand. So it was isolating at times.

The discomfort that Garces-Foley describes is clearly evident here. It is not that people don't appreciate the vision of a multicultural community, but rather that there are many bridges to cross, many uncomfortable situations to negotiate, many potential conflicts to work through. It requires a commitment, a decision in one's mind that 'I am going to do this!' It can be a step of faith to make oneself vulnerable to others and the process can become emotionally wearing, yet Volf also points to the potential for transformation that can emerge from such an embrace. Consider this story someone once told me of the unexpected outcome of a church social event held at a ten-pin bowling centre:

> I think one of the things that different cultures have brought into the church is their warmth and their openness to express their love for you by hugs and things like that. Whereas before it was a bit of a no-go area in our church, that's softened even the hardest of hearts. Loretta was telling me that Jane had said something to her and Loretta said, 'I'd really like to invite her round but I don't think she'll come to my house.' I said, 'Why not?' Loretta saw a different side of Jane and Jane saw a different side of Loretta and it was really funny the sort of relationship that was struck up out of that evening.

Here the warmth of friendship, and an atmosphere of physical embrace, has led to a deeper embrace which has helped to overcome prejudices and foster reconciliation. It takes time, and in the case of Loretta and Jane it is an embrace that will develop gradually, but the developing relationship has the potential to produce dividends both for them personally and for the church fellowship as a whole.

In withdrawing from the embrace, what remains is recognition of the other person's uniqueness: not an attempt to ignore ethnic distinctions but rather an appreciation of one another's distinctiveness. Some may have achieved reconciliation and a healing of wounds, since many come with stories of racism and prejudice of different orders. Hurtful things are said in any church community, sometimes unwittingly and sometimes deliberately, and the potential for misunderstanding increases when people of differing ethnic backgrounds come together. However, for all who embrace there is a bridging of cultures, a deepening sense of being the people of God together and of connection with the divine community that is the Trinity.

Not everyone finds it easy to make new friendships, and even those who do can struggle in a multicultural environment. Those who are easily able to facilitate conversations and relationships across ethnic boundaries are important people in the church. The national bird of Jamaica is the swallow-tail hummingbird. One of the distinctive characteristics of the hummingbird is that it cross-pollinates, taking nectar from brightly coloured flowers, but also carrying pollen from one to another, enabling those flowers to bear fruit and reproduce. This makes it an ideal symbol for a nation whose motto is 'out of many, one people'. In a church setting where one of the purposes of meeting is to grow together in love and fellowship, hummingbird-type people who can naturally connect and foster friendships are vital. Garces-Foley, looking from a sociological perspective, observes that though many people choose to be with others of a similar ethnic or cultural background, there are people who actually prefer diverse settings and seek out cross-cultural encounters and friendships. She notes that such people will form social connections on the basis of other factors such as class, age, professional status and educational background (Garces-Foley, 2007, p. 130).

Washington and Kehrein speak of the need to empower and appreciate the reconcilers in the church, those people who have the gift and the passion to foster cross-cultural relationships and to encourage those who are wary of becoming too involved to be more open to others. Such people can help those, often of differing cultural backgrounds, who have the skills but are often overlooked for roles in church life, to begin to work with others in teams (Washington and Kehrein, 1993, pp. 209–20).

Other people who help to transcend ethnic and cultural boundaries are those who are willing to come and express to the leadership the needs of particular ethnic communities.

Sometimes people from different ethnic backgrounds can be reluctant to approach the leaders directly. This may be for a number of reasons: they may feel unsure about the way of doing things; they may lack confidence in speaking English; they may see the church leader as too important to approach directly because of the conventions within their own culture (something we will consider in Chapter 8). The matter in question may be simply the sharing of information or the suggestion that a leader might go and visit a family who need help. It could be that a relative in someone's wider family or home country has died and the person concerned is looking for spiritual support – perhaps a prayer in their home at a gathering of their friends and relatives as they grieve. It can seem strange to a British church leader when someone functions as a go-between, but rather than a problem this can be seen as an opportunity to provide better pastoral care, to build better cross-cultural relationships and, over time, stronger direct relationships with members of the cultural group concerned. When I have been able to respond to an individual's need on one or two occasions, having been alerted to it by the go-between, it has paved the way for that person to begin to come to me directly, and so allowed the multicultural dimensions of pastoral care among the congregation to develop.

Friendship

If a healthy supportive environment in a multicultural church is successfully nurtured it will be because people of differing ethnic backgrounds have moved beyond being acquaintances at church for Sunday services to become genuine friends. A story from the landmark 1910 World Missionary Conference held in Edinburgh illustrates this for us. The conference brought together 1,215 representatives, most of whom were from North America and Europe. However, 19 of those attending were from the non-Western world, and they included Bishop V. S. Azariah from India.

Azariah's speech is one of the best remembered of the 1910 conference. He had been recommended to the conference by Henry Whitehead, the Anglo-Catholic Bishop of Madras, and was accompanied on the journey by the bishop's wife, Isabel. Unfortunately, whereas she stayed in expensive hotels en route, he was booked into cheaper accommodation; she travelled in second-class carriages on trains, while he was allocated a seat in third class. Azariah was troubled that the patronage of the West was one-sided and that people like himself were not being treated as equals in the Church. In his speech he drew attention to Ephesians 3.18–19, saying 'It is only "with all the Saints" that we can comprehend the love of Christ which passeth knowledge, that we might be filled with all the fullness of God". This will be possible only from spiritual friendships between the two races.' He went on to say, 'Through all the ages to come the Indian Church will rise up in gratitude to attest the heroism and self-denying labours of the missionary body. You have given your goods to feed the poor. You have given your bodies to be burned. We also ask for love. Give us friends!' (Stanley, 2009, p. 125).

Azariah's plea to be treated not as an inferior but as a friend is a powerful call to us to overcome the fears and prejudices within multicultural churches that we hardly know are there. It presents a challenge, too, for the leaders of our churches to make friends with other church leaders of different ethnic and cultural backgrounds from their own. This should happen both within the denominations and church networks we belong to and beyond; it should entail searching out neighbouring churches, whether they have their own buildings or whether they rent schools or halls each Sunday. We should make efforts to do this not only for the sake of the unity of the Church, but also because as we develop the diversity of our own friendships it will help us both to understand people from differing cultural backgrounds and to become more effective in our everyday pastoral work.

8

Developing diverse leadership teams

One of the significant challenges for the leaders of churches in multicultural contexts is how to develop diverse leadership teams. In Chapter 5 we saw how important it is to develop diverse teams as part of a strategy to overcome prejudice. However, even with a wholehearted commitment to do this, it can be very difficult to achieve.

Delbert Sandiford notes research undertaken in the diocese of Southwark which showed the great disparity that can exist between the proportion of black and minority ethnic (BME) people on church councils and on the electoral roll. There were many churches with ethnically diverse congregations but this diversity was not reflected where the power in the church lay (Sandiford, 2010, p. 18).

Discussions emerging from this research identified two critical barriers which made it difficult for such people to take up positions of responsibility. The first was that BME people were likely to be more recent arrivals to the churches and often lacked awareness of how church governance works. Second, models of leadership and governance differed widely between countries and cultures even within the same church denomination, and so information was needed to enable BME people to function effectively in churches in Britain.

In a more recent study, Anglican cleric Andy Jolley laments the fact that 'In the growing number of ethnically diverse churches and communities, especially in the inner cities, church leaders are still frequently white. Despite concerted attempts at encouraging black and minority ethnic people into church leadership, progress has been stubbornly slow' (Jolley, 2015, p. 10).

He also identifies two barriers that work to inhibit progress in this area. The first is the emphasis, still prevalent in many churches, on having one trained, ordained vicar, minister or leader. He observes that in Scripture, plural leadership in local churches was more typical and that such a model offers a way forward for increasing participation. The second barrier is that in multi-ethnic urban churches it is often the white middle class, who may be commuting in from the suburbs, who carry much of the responsibility for children's work, preaching, the provision of music and other ministries. There is no doubt that such long-distance commitment to inner city churches, often because of a previous connection, provides much-needed resources both in ministry and finance; however, Jolley rightly argues that there is a need to encourage, mentor and develop potential leaders from within the local community who may be more likely to be from differing ethnic and socio-economic backgrounds.

Those who are familiar with ministry in multicultural contexts will not disagree with either Sandiford's or Jolley's analysis of the problems. Both moreover point to the need to be intentional in taking affirmative action in identifying and training potential leaders, and in increasing the awareness among existing church leaders of the need to mentor, train and encourage BME candidates from differing ethnic backgrounds. This is, however, no easy task – it takes time and commitment before results begin to be seen.

Empowering leaders: Monica's story

The following story illustrates a number of issues that arise when we seek to empower people of differing ethnic backgrounds within a church. The story emerges from a congregational church, but will be insightful for all who are attempting to raise leaders in any context.

The church needed a new administrator, which was a voluntary role whose incumbent was appointed by the congregation. The leaders discussed what possible candidates there were among the people of the church. What became clear very quickly was that the leadership team, made up of white men, were coming up only with the names of other white men. So the minister suggested Monica. The reply from the others was unanimous, 'Who is Monica?' Monica was a black woman, originally from an island in the Caribbean, who had attended the church for over ten years. The issue was left for prayer and consideration.

Another leadership team meeting came around and again time was spent considering possible new administrators. The same names were raised and the minister asked again, 'What about Monica?' The reply this time was, 'Is she able to do the job?' The reply was that she was a committed Christian, had been a midwife for many years, was secretary of her allotment club and worked in a voluntary role in administration for a local Christian charity. She was also retired and had some time on her hands. It seemed evident that she was eminently equipped to do the job; indeed she was better placed, overall, than the other candidates who had been mentioned.

When, at the next leadership team meeting, the issue was raised once more the reply was different: 'Maybe Monica would be a good choice.' Monica was duly put forward to the congregation, elected to the position and served the church well.

This example exposes a major issue that can arise when we seek to develop a healthy, well-integrated multicultural church. For the leadership team, existing friendships with those similar to themselves and preconceived notions regarding what a 'good' church administrator would look like had led them to have too narrow a focus on who would be suitable. Monica didn't look like the administrators the church had known before, even though on paper she was a match for any of them. It was also the case that, because of her cultural background, Monica wasn't known to those in leadership in the same way as others. The leadership team was a good one, open and committed to developing a healthy multicultural church, but because of their lack of familiarity with members of the congregation from differing ethnic backgrounds and their expectations of what a new administrator might look like, there was effectively a glass ceiling within the congregation which acted to prevent people of certain ethnic and cultural backgrounds becoming leaders.

This kind of situation can lead to what is known as institutional racism. Institutional racism occurs when, although individuals are not necessarily acting in ways that could be described as racist, the cumulative effect of the systems and procedures within an institution means that certain people are excluded simply because of who they are.

Sandiford highlights the issue that even when we are successful in appointing people to key positions of responsibility in the church, such appointments may not prove successful in the long term if those concerned feel like fish out of water in the roles they find themselves in. This can happen, not because the person appointed is unable to fulfil the role, but because the environment he or she has entered is so culturally bound that it is as if a language is being spoken of which the person knows very little. Leaders need to become more aware of intercultural issues in order to avoid such matters leading to frustration or conflict. It is impossible to learn everything there is to know about every ethnicity or nationality, but Geert Hofstede's analysis of cultures provides a way of assessing potential conflicts in any leadership team.

Hofstede's analysis of cultures

Within the context of a multinational computer industry, Dutch social psychologist Hofstede has devoted his career to an investigation of national cultural differences, and in the more recent editions of his work he has collaborated with both his son, Gert Jan Hofstede, and the Bulgarian researcher Michael Minkov, who have contributed to the development of his ideas. He describes culture as 'the collective programming of the mind that distinguishes the members of one group or category of people from others' (Hofstede, Hofstede and Minkov, 2010, p. 6). With regard to cross-cultural relations, Hofstede acknowledges four problem areas emerging from studies by social psychologists; they are (Hofstede, Hofstede and Minkov, 2010, p. 30):[1]

- relation to authority;
- conception of self in the relationship between the individual and society;
- conception of self in the individual's concept of masculinity and femininity;
- ways of dealing with conflict.

Drawing on this work and developing his own analysis of national cultures from extensive data, he identifies four 'dimensions of cultures', describing a dimension as 'an aspect of a culture that can be measured relative to other cultures'. He names these dimensions of cultures 'power distance', 'collectivism versus individualism', 'femininity versus masculinity' and 'uncertainty avoidance' (Hofstede, Hofstede and Minkov, 2010, p. 31).

Power distance

Power distance is a measure of the emotional distance that separates subordinates from their bosses. Hofstede's power distance index is drawn from research exploring the extent to which employees were afraid to express disagreement with their managers. It includes consideration of employees' perception of their boss's decision-making style. He writes,

> In small-power-distance countries, there is limited dependence of subordinates on bosses, and there is a preference for consultation (that is, interdependence among boss and subordinate). The emotional distance between them is relatively small: subordinates will rather easily approach and contradict their

bosses. In large-power-distance countries, there is considerable dependence of subordinates on bosses. Subordinates respond by either preferring such dependence (in the form of an autocratic or paternalistic boss) or rejecting it entirely ... known as counter-dependence ... Large-power-distance countries thus show a pattern of polarization between dependence and counter-dependence. In these cases the emotional distance between subordinates and their bosses is large: subordinates are unlikely to approach and contradict their bosses directly.

(Hofstede, Hofstede and Minkov, 2010, p. 61)

Countries showing a small power distance (SPD) include Austria, Scandinavian countries and the UK. Countries showing a large power distance (LPD) include Russia, West African countries, China and India.

It is not difficult to see how and why problems emerge when people from LPD countries begin to live and relate within a SPD country such as the UK. Take for instance a church council or leadership meeting in the UK where there are people present of diverse backgrounds but with a British person chairing the meeting. The chair may well want to work collaboratively and may find that those who are used to this way of working make a substantial contribution, agreeing or disagreeing with the person in charge and sharing their own opinions. At the same time, others who originate from LPD countries may be expecting the leader to make the decisions and may be reluctant to contribute their own opinion unless directly asked. They will not wish to be disrespectful to those in authority, and if asked their personal opinion they may express their view in roundabout ways to avoid conflict.

Conversely, imagine the same meeting chaired by a church leader from a LPD country, used to making unilateral decisions and expecting unquestioning loyalty. Such a person may find it difficult to understand why others on the committee are raising contrary views. They will appear to be rebels, complain of a lack of consultation and may, if their views are not considered, eventually leave the church to find a spiritual home which, culturally, seems more familiar to them. It has often been observed that some white people will leave a church if a new vicar or minister is appointed who is black; they struggle with the unfamiliarity of the new church leader's cultural style, even though a BME leader from a LPD culture will at the same time be carrying on his or her own struggle with the traditional British cultural style.

Resolving cultural differences of this kind requires patience, clarity and a willingness to be vulnerable, that is to say how one is feeling. There is a need to go beyond the factual to appreciate people's emotional state. Hofstede describes power distance as an 'emotional distance', and it is by becoming vulnerable emotionally that the distance can be bridged. A willingness to engage at a deeper level is likely to develop better understanding and pave the way for strategies for working together well to emerge. For example, the following conversation is based on an encounter with someone from a LPD culture in a committee meeting:

ME: So, James, what do you think about this issue?
JAMES: Well, I am happy to go along with what people
        think we should do.
ME: Yes, but I would be interested to hear what you think,
        looking at the issue from your cultural point of view.
JAMES: (tells a story of something that happened in his
        home country)
ME: So I think you are saying that you would do
        something different.
JAMES: I am happy to go along with what others think.
ME: But I think what you are saying is important for
        us to hear and maybe we need to hold off making
        a decision.

Afterwards, James told me how hard it was for him to speak against what the pastor was saying and said he would be happy with whatever was decided. I assured him his participation in the meeting and his opinion and insights were really important to us and would help us make better decisions. It takes time, but better understanding of others' emotional approach to these situations helps to bridge the power distance and develop respectful but collaborative ways of working together in leadership teams.

These differences express themselves in other ways. For example, British people often use first names when speaking to their church leader, whereas those from other cultures may prefer to show deference by using titles such as 'Father', 'Pastor' and so on. Approaches towards raising children differ: those from SPD cultures expect their children to become independent whereas those from LPD cultures expect their children to remain interdependent, offering lifelong respect towards those older than themselves or who are of higher status. Approaches to children's work in church differ too, depending on whether the expectation is for the children to be treated as equals and to participate in their learning (evident in new, inclusive ways of doing church popular in the UK such as 'All-age worship' or 'Messy Church') or for them to sit quietly and listen to the much wiser and more learned adults, an approach to learning which to the British appears old-fashioned.

Here the insights of Allport in Chapter 5 can usefully be applied. Encouraging people of differing ethnic backgrounds to work together in a team responsible for some small area of the children's work may prove more difficult to begin with, but can pay dividends over time. If people are willing to work together and allow friendship to develop, if the vision of the church's multicultural development is clear and the support of the church leader evident, then in the longer term such conflict of styles can be overcome, creating synergy in this area of church ministry.

An interesting footnote to Hofstede's research in the area of power distance is that in small-power-distance cultures such as

Britain it was found that those who were of lower social status and poorer education produced power distance scores nearly as high as those in large-power-distance cultures. As Hofstede states, 'working class families often have a large-power-distance subculture' (Hofstede, Hofstede and Minkov, 2010, p. 71). This observation resonates with the experience of those leading churches in working-class or low-income environments, where the congregation often depend on the leader of the church to make decisions and lead the church without expecting to participate in any way in the decision-making process. This may be because of their lack of experience in management and therefore a lack of confidence in their ability to make decisions, or it may simply be a lack of interest in what are perceived to be tedious processes which they have no intrinsic desire to be a part of. Whatever the reason, the effect is that such people become excluded from the important decision-making processes within church life.

When people from SPD cultures and LPD cultures come together, the risk is that power struggles will emerge as those from each culture find it difficult to understand or trust one another. This can appear to be a racist conflict, but although racism may inevitably be a part of it, it also reflects the misunderstandings and conflict engendered by differing cultural approaches towards those in authority. Leaders in multicultural churches need to give time to building good relationships, carefully observe the dynamics within their team, and encourage open and honest reflection on how different members of the leadership team are relating together and to members of the church.

Collectivism versus individualism

The second dimension of culture which Hofstede identifies is 'collectivism versus individualism':

> The vast majority of people in our world live in societies in which the interest of the group prevails over the interest of the

individual. We will call these societies collectivist … the 'we' group (or in-group) is the major source of one's identity and the only secure protection one has against the hardships of life. Therefore, one owes lifelong loyalty to one's in-group, and breaking this loyalty is one of the worst things a person can do …

A minority of people in our world live in societies in which the interests of the individual prevail over the interests of the group, societies that we will call individualist … This 'I', their personal identity, is distinct from other people's 'I's, and these others are classified not according to their group membership but instead according to individual characteristics.

(Hofstede, Hofstede and Minkov, 2010, pp. 90–1)

Hofstede observes a strong correlation between LPD and collectivism and similarly between SPD and individualism: 'In cultures in which people are dependent on 'in-groups' these people are usually also dependent on power figures … In cultures in which people are relatively independent from in-groups, they are usually also less dependent on powerful others' (Hofstede, Hofstede and Minkov, 2010, pp. 103–4).

Given that Britain is very firmly in the individualist dimension of culture and countries such as China, Pakistan and those of West Africa are all equally firmly in the collectivist dimension, this contrast between worldviews is very evident. People from collectivist cultures often work long hours, sending money to their home country to support their extended families. They will tend to avoid direct confrontation in order to avoid offence and wish to avoid bringing shame upon the family. In contrast, those from individualist cultures will tend to be independent of their nuclear family and become self-supporting as soon as is practical. They will find virtue in speaking their mind.

In church life these differences can express themselves in the understanding of church itself. British people often see church as an organization that needs to be run well, whereas those from collectivist cultures see church as a family where everyone has responsibility for one another (and their children) in the same way as if they were one large extended family. If a British person feels let down by his or her church it is seen as a failure of the system ('we need to organize our pastoral care more effectively'), whereas if a person from a collectivist culture feels let down it will be more personal ('where were you?'). British people tend to back off from being too personally involved, whereas people from collectivist cultures tend to have a greater expectation that others among their wider circle of family and friends will be ready to help out. A couple having marital difficulties or, as parents, struggling with the behaviour of a child may, in a collectivist culture, expect their church leader or a trusted uncle to be involved in helping with the situation. In an individualist culture others looking on may feel that it is best not to get involved, and that the couple need to work things out for themselves.

The tension that may arise between those from individualist cultures and those from collectivist cultures can lead to the development of cliques. Those from collectivist cultures find their support among people like themselves and may have little or no expectation of others in their church community. It can take many years for a leader from an individualist culture to build up trust with collectivist people groups and be invited to share in their cultural gatherings. For example, as discussed in Chapter 7, the practice in a number of Caribbean countries when a person dies is to have a gathering on the ninth night after the death. This may be a social gathering but may also include songs, readings and prayers. A church leader of a different cultural group may or may not be invited to attend and take part. Unless good relationships have been developed, those from individualist cultures may feel they lack the communal cultural awareness to confidently become involved and can feel that those from collectivist cultures keep themselves to themselves.

The tension that can arise when cliques develop can be overcome if all members of the community are able to learn from one another. Individualists can benefit from developing a stronger sense of community and family in church life, while collectivists can work to create space for such people to become a part of their ethnically orientated community life. Developing multi-ethnic rather than mono-ethnic teams and groups in church life can also help to build rapport and understanding among those of differing ethnic backgrounds rather than encouraging cliquishness.

Femininity versus masculinity

The third dimension of culture which Hofstede discovered was the extent to which a society exhibits feminine or masculine virtues. He defines such attributes in this way:

> A society is called masculine when emotional gender roles are clearly distinct: men are supposed to be assertive, tough, and focused on material success, whereas women are supposed to be more modest, tender, and concerned with the quality of life. A society is called feminine when emotional gender roles overlap: both men and women are supposed to be modest, tender, and concerned with the quality of life.
>
> (Hofstede, Hofstede and Minkov, 2010, p. 140)

In Hofstede's research, countries such as Jamaica, the UK, the USA, Poland and China showed as being more masculine under his definition. In contrast, the Scandinavian countries showed as being more feminine, and areas such as West and East Africa were in the middle, though slightly towards the feminine end of the scale. Essentially a country is defined as being more feminine if male and female roles are interchangeable, whereas it is defined as being more masculine if gender roles are more clearly defined and reinforced at all levels of society.

This is an interesting aspect of Hofstede's research, because although Britain is identified as being at the masculine end of the scale, in reality churches are split between those affirming complementary roles for men and women and those who see men and women's roles as interchangeable, and which would therefore be identified as being more feminine. Given the diversity in this area that already exists within churches in Britain, the increased diversity of cultural habits brought by those of different ethnic backgrounds only makes the issue more complex.

The tension that can arise out of this within the local church comes from stereotyping. As we discussed in Chapter 5, stereotyping occurs when an individual has cast in his or her mind how a particular person from another culture may act or react, without taking the time to discover that person's reactions first hand. Stereotyping persists when, despite information to the contrary, the assumptions cast are allowed to remain. Take, for example, West African-led churches. White British people may assume that they would be masculine in character, perceiving strong black African men who appear to be dominant in their communities. However, Hofstede's research suggests that they would be more neutral, if not a little towards the feminine side within his matrix of definition. In reality there are many West African-led churches whose pastors are women. It is also true that the wives of male African pastors are often held in much higher regard than a white British vicar or pastor's wife may be. And the emphasis on community within a LPD culture can mean that West African male pastors play a benevolent role in the community, enabling people to be cared and provided for, their children encouraged into university and wayward young people mentored in a way that white British church leaders rarely do. Reflecting on Hofstede's description of the masculine–feminine dimension can reveal insights beyond the stereotypes that are often played out in British church life.

The opportunity for growth here is for a church leader to become more inclusive in his or her approach as to who takes responsibility in the church, engendering an inclusive and nurturing dynamic within church life. A multicultural church, in its ambition to become more inclusive and embrace the potential that people of differing ethnic backgrounds can bring, will inevitably lean towards becoming feminine by Hofstede's definition. It will encourage the interchangeability of roles, which will be transformative for those from cultural backgrounds where roles are more clearly defined. This area will be one in which British culture may be influenced by the presence of those from other cultures.

One biblical precedent which resonates with this dynamic is the encounter of Jesus with the Samaritan woman in John 4. There we see how Jesus responds in such a way as to confound the Samaritan woman's expectations. She herself has probably been abused by men who ought to have protected her. So she expects hostility from Jesus. Instead Jesus' response is one of compassion and tenderness; he treats her as someone who has untapped potential. The result is that she becomes an evangelist within her own village and Jesus spends two days there, transforming the lives of many of the inhabitants. Instead of acting according to a masculine stereotype, and as a result stereotyping the Samaritan woman, Jesus shows a feminine side, including her among his friends and followers and enlarging the circle of those who believe in him.

Avoidance of uncertainty

The fourth dimension of culture that Hofstede draws from his research is uncertainty avoidance, which he defines·as 'the extent to which the members of a culture feel threatened by ambiguous or unknown situations' (Hofstede, Hofstede and Minkov, 2010, p. 191). This relates to the anxiety that will typically be felt by a people of a particular nation when faced with uncertainty. Those who were found in the research to cope more easily were the inhabitants of countries such as the UK, India, China, and the African countries; places whose inhabitants coped less easily included France, Germany, Russia, eastern European countries and some in South America.

This dimension of culture manifests itself in a variety of ways. First, Hofstede notes, 'anxious cultures tend to be expressive cultures. They are the places where people talk with their hands and where it is socially acceptable to raise one's voice, to show one's emotions and to pound the table' (Hofstede, Hofstede and Minkov, 2010, p. 196). Conversely, in weak uncertainty-avoidance countries, 'Aggression and emotions are not supposed to be shown: people who behave emotionally or noisily meet with social disapproval. This means that stress cannot be released in activity; it has to be internalized' (Hofstede, Hofstede and Minkov, 2010, p. 196). Members of anxious cultures set out to avoid uncertainty by bringing issues and potential conflicts to the surface so that they can be worked through to avoid ambiguity. Those in non-anxious cultures can live with ambiguity and so often leave things unsaid to avoid conflict.

A second expression of uncertainty avoidance in cultures shows itself in how people learn. Those from cultures with a greater avoidance of uncertainty will feel more comfortable in situations in which there is a correct answer and prefer to learn from teachers who sound like experts and can give them the correct answers. On the other hand, those from cultures with a lower avoidance of uncertainty will enjoy being rewarded for originality in their answer and prefer to learn from teachers who can admit the limits of their knowledge and are able to explain difficult concepts in simple terms.

A third expression is that a culture with a high degree of uncertainty avoidance will have an emotional attachment to rules, believing that 'Matters that can be structured should not be left to chance' (Hofstede, Hofstede and Minkov, 2010, p. 209). This can lead to a commitment to formal structures regardless of their usefulness or efficiency. Those belonging to cultures with a low degree of uncertainty avoidance will be less attached to the need for rules, though this often means that there are more unwritten rules which those from other cultures may struggle to negotiate.

It is evident from these three expressions of uncertainty avoidance that if there is a mix of cultures within a church committee or leadership team, then misunderstandings can readily occur. Team members who express their views animatedly, wanting to thrash things out, may well leave those who would prefer to avoid conflict feeling harassed. Similarly, those from cultures with an expectation of teaching or preaching with certainties may be frustrated to encounter a style of teaching which is more questioning, or involves discussion or participation. When a difficult theological issue arose in the church, I found that, in general, people from cultures with a higher uncertainty avoidance were much more likely to want the church to be specific regarding what we believed and to ensure dissenters would fall in line, whereas in general, the white British people were more willing to proceed with a certain amount of ambiguity. Both approaches have their downsides, and so it is not that one way is better than another. The point is simply that when operating within a multicultural community, a church leader may find it more difficult to navigate such issues.

There are numerous ways in which conflict and misunderstandings can occur in a multicultural context but once again there is, as in the other dimensions of culture, the opportunity for growth. This opportunity comes from an increasing maturity in expressing opinions, thoughts and feelings within committees and among teams, and recognizing that whereas it can be helpful for some people to be focused and specific in the process of decision making, multicultural churches are, by their very nature, unpredictable and adaptable communities. An effective multicultural church leader needs to be able to ease anxieties, encourage participation and lead diverse groups to settled, clearly understood, and shared decisions.

What makes a good leader of a multicultural church?

Hofstede's analysis of cultures offers a useful matrix to help make sense of the unpredictable dynamics that can arise in multicultural committees or leadership teams. It is not that one needs to know where a particular nationality or culture fits in the matrix (though Hofstede offers that information). People do not all behave the same way within a culture, even though common traits are evident among them. The benefit of Hofstede's analysis is that it enables a church leader to understand how and why people from different ethnic backgrounds differ in their approach, and to identify potential conflicts and develop strategies to avoid, overcome or grow through such threats to the well-being of the committee or team.

It is important for church leaders not to be bound by Hofstede's analysis but rather to see that, equipped with his insights, we have an opportunity to help all members of our committees or leadership teams understand one another better and work to their strengths. There are numerous ways in which conflict and misunderstandings can occur in a multicultural context, but there is also the opportunity for growth. Multicultural churches are, by their very nature, unpredictable and adaptable communities. A good leader of a multicultural church will be able to:

1 model and encourage vulnerable leadership which will enable the emotional distances between people of differing cultures to be understood and bridged;
2 foster friendship, loyalty and concern for one another which will enable the widening of the collectivist approach to community from one cultural group to the church as a whole;
3 encourage the interchangeability of roles, ensuring that inclusivity in terms of ethnicity is accompanied by the inclusion of women, people from differing socio-economic backgrounds, and others who may be marginalized within church life;
4 show patience and clarity when discussing difficult issues, ensuring that all feel able to participate openly and contribute to any decisions made.

9

Growing in mission

———•◆•———

Developing healthy multicultural churches is not an end in itself but is intended to enable the local church to better fulfil its mission in the world. By mission I mean establishing the kingdom of God in its broadest sense, with the conviction that multicultural churches have a unique opportunity at this point in the history of humankind. This chapter explores how developing multiculturally enables and enhances the mission of the Church in four ways: expressing the transforming love of God through unity, advocating for justice, facilitating both personal and church renewal, and enabling church growth in the context of multicultural communities.

Mission as unity

Church unity is a theme that echoes throughout Scripture. 'How good and pleasant it is when God's people live together in unity!' (Psalm 133) declares the psalmist. Jesus prays 'for those who will believe in me through their message, that all of them may be one, Father, just as you are in me and I am in you' (John 17.20–21). Jesus also specifically links unity to the witness of the Church when he says, 'A new command I give you: love one another. As I have loved you, so you must love one another. By this everyone will know that you are my disciples, if you love one another' (John 13.34–35). In the early Church, Paul encouraged the Christians in Ephesus: 'Be completely humble and gentle; be patient, bearing with one another in love. Make every effort to keep the unity of the Spirit through the bond of peace'

(Ephesians 4.2–3). The presence of healthy multicultural congregations is itself a witness to the transforming love of God. When people of such disparate backgrounds are seen to be able to share life together despite all their differences, it is a visible sign of their unity in Christ and demonstrates the power of his love.

A more challenging aspect of unity is to bring church leaders and congregations together as a public demonstration of the body of Christ in a particular locality. For example, my local church leaders' group has good representation from the traditional mainstream denominations (Anglican, Baptist, Methodist and Roman Catholic), but it has always proved difficult to draw into this fellowship leaders from other congregations who may be meeting in their own premises, church halls, community halls and so on. One reason for this may be that many of these leaders also have full- or part-time jobs other than their church ministry, and are not available during the day when the meetings often take place. However, there are also other reasons. A Chinese pastor I spoke to described how church leaders from some cultures find the British habit of small-talk at such meetings difficult to understand. He and others like him wondered what the point of the meeting was if they only talked about the weather! The culture of building relationships through what appear to be rather trivial conversations, paving the way for more significant engagement that may arise out of these relationships, is probably one of the unwritten codes of conduct in the UK.

As well as the conflict over ways of engaging, there are often differences in the style of worship, ways of doing church, and theology between congregations which can make church leaders wary of each other. Beyond this, some church leaders lack the vision to develop friendships with other local church leaders and prefer to concentrate on maintaining the success and growth of their own church. Sri Lankan theologian Vinoth Ramachandra emphasizes the importance of unity among ethnically diverse Christians, saying, 'mission is not primarily about going. Nor is mission primarily about doing anything. Mission is about being. It is about being a distinctive kind of people, a countercultural, multinational community among the nations. It is modelling before a sceptical world what the living God of the Bible really is like' (Peskett and Ramachandra, 2003, p. 123).

When church leaders from diverse backgrounds do gather, such unity often emerges from collective activity in the local community, such as food banks, soup kitchens, night shelters, street pastors and liaison with the council over issues of mutual concern. Some of the most meaningful times when we have stood together with Christians from many different churches and differing ethnic backgrounds have been the thanksgiving services that follow a season of serving together in the community. However, there needs to be more intentional reaching out to and engaging with one another. There is an opportunity here for churches whose halls are used by other congregations to collaborate on a mission or community project that will help foster friendships, trust and fellowship between the two congregations. Such activity may well help pave the way for more meaningful sharing of worship.

Church leaders can benefit personally from developing cross-cultural friendships with other church leaders in their locality. If activity together helps to build relationships (one of Gordon Allport's observations, noted in Chapter 5) then church leaders need to build on that to develop mutual, respectful friendships. Such friendships encourage the unity of the Church and lead to mutually beneficial relationships. These in turn may, over time, extend from gatherings of leaders towards the engagement of congregations, and this investment in relationships can also help congregations to find joy and strength in working and witnessing to Christ together.

Mission as justice

The diversity of people in a multicultural church brings to the fore issues of justice. Author Brian McLaren describes justice as 'the right use of power in our relationships with others' (McLaren, Padilla and Seeber, 2009, p. 22) and a leader of a multicultural church will be drawn in to issues of justice in two different ways: as an advocate to those suffering injustice and as the lead campaigner on issues of justice within the church.

We discussed the issue of racism in Chapter 7, but in the role of advocate the leaders of multicultural churches may find themselves supporting members of the church who are facing discrimination outside the church, whether at work, at school or in their neighbourhood. If the church leader is white and has not experienced prejudice personally, then he or she will have to be particularly careful to listen to the complaint and try to step into the shoes of the person involved. It can be too easy to feel that a fuss is being made about nothing. Kumar Rajagopalan, Regional Minister for Racial Justice in the London Baptist Association, questions the extent to which white church leaders have understood the privilege they continue to hold in the balance of power. He writes, 'when the powerful White middle class tell BME communities that their quest for justice has been achieved, that is often indicative of the fact that no progress has been made. Essentially, it is tantamount to the fact that there has been no shift in power. The master–servant relationship still prevails' (Rajagopalan, 2015, p. 185). It is important to allow those who have been discriminated against to articulate their complaint and explain how they feel. They will probably have experienced discrimination many times, and so when a particular incident returns it to the surface, they will bring to it an accumulation of grief which, while it focuses the anger and protest, may also mean that they need someone who is willing to listen, believe in them and offer support.

Visa issues are significant for many in multicultural churches. As an advocate, the church leader may be asked to support a member of the congregation who is applying for residency in the UK. The legal process is often lengthy and can be immensely frustrating, and there is so much at stake for the person or family involved that it becomes emotionally draining. Immigration is such a hotly contested political issue that the process of seeking residency can inevitably leave the person feeling she is the victim of prejudice. Tribunals and appeals add to the feeling of hostility and conflict in this process, and the presence of a church leader will be a support to the person and may help to ensure the case is dealt with fairly.

Another way that a church leader may become an advocate for justice is with regard to family issues. For example, young people whose parents are from one culture and who have themselves been raised within British culture find themselves caught between two cultures, complicating what can already be a tumultuous time in their lives. Sometimes the parents decide that their son or daughter ought to spend time abroad so that he or she can learn the traditional values of the parents' culture, and that may lead to dissension in the family home. Being sensitive to the traditions of the parents, exercising pastoral care and yet being an advocate for the young to allow their voice to be heard is an uncomfortable place to stand. If the conflict becomes inflamed, then the church leader needs to be ready to attempt to ease the tension or raise the alarm.

Polygamy is prevalent in some cultures, and some in our churches may have had fathers or grandfathers for whom it was considered normal. When such families became Christians the subsequent generations largely moved on from that practice, but its legacy may still influence men today in their attitudes towards women. Marriage enhancement seminars and programmes raising awareness of issues with respect to the rights of women may be important tools in helping us deal with these situations, both across the cultures in church life and indeed within the wider British culture too.

Churches regularly support campaigns run by charities highlighting issues abroad, often offering financial assistance and occasionally petitioning local MPs to put pressure on the UK government to act. In multicultural churches such issues may have affected people in the congregation, and one ought to be careful not to pontificate regarding an issue in a particular country when someone from that country is present, may have experienced the issue first hand, and yet has not been consulted. On one occasion our local ecumenical service for the Week of Prayer for Christian Unity had been written by people from India and circulated from a central source. It struck me afterwards that although Indians were present in the churches involved, no one had thought to consult them or involve them before using the material. It seemed, on reflection, a strange state of affairs to be depending on materials distributed from a central source to inform us about the church in India when there were people in our churches who could tell us about it first hand.

I have known people in the churches I have served who lost relatives in civil wars and conflicts, who have experienced violence and the impact of violence, who have been raised under the suspicion of oppressive regimes because of their faith or their family's position in society and who have experienced the effects of corruption. There have also been those who have suffered as a result of the impact of disease, such as HIV & AIDS or Ebola. There is opportunity in all of these situations to inform the congregation with first-hand examples and, when appropriate, to campaign to improve life in the countries or regions affected.

Church leaders have the opportunity to campaign on issues which have cultural elements to them and may resonate with people in our churches from the parts of the world concerned. For example, slavery in the UK today sees people trafficked from countries such as Romania, Albania, Nigeria, Vietnam and China. People in poverty are lured into the promise of a better life, only to find themselves entrapped into forced working conditions with no means of escape. A total of 1,746 cases were reported in the UK in 2013, though the real figure is thought to be much higher. Another example, female genital mutilation/

cutting (FGM/C) involves the circumcision of girls and young women, with no known benefits but causing hugely damaging emotional, psychological and physical scars. Campaigner Elaine Storkey notes:

> Most of the practice is concentrated in 26 African nations, but with migration the practice occurs now in every part of the globe ... A report on FGM issued by the UK government in 2014 suggested that around 140,000 women in England and Wales are living with the consequences of FGM and around 10,000 girls under the age of 15 are likely to undergo cutting.
>
> (Storkey, 2015, pp. 29–30)

Often thought to be a problem within Islam, FGM/C is in fact a cultural practice which precedes Islam; though it mainly affects Muslims, Christian women from the regions where it is part of the culture can suffer too (Storkey, 2015, pp. 42–3).

A congregation can immediately support campaigns to educate and overcome such practices. However, some issues of justice are more difficult to negotiate in multicultural churches. Many see the advocacy of same-sex marriage as an issue of justice and there are strong feelings regarding the issue, some in favour and many against. Within the Anglican communion, views on the matter vary across the world and cultural differences have emerged in the ensuing discussions and debates. These differences can be apparent within the local church too and although it is not entirely a cultural issue (within the British Church generally there is a variety of different views on the issue), any discussion of it becomes more complex within a multicultural church. We cannot assume a neo-colonial spirit which says that the West is best placed to find the way forward in this and other matters, but instead would benefit from listening deeply, facilitating constructive dialogue, seeking to understand those of differing ethnic backgrounds and pursuing the demands of love and faithfulness, justice and mercy together. Bhikhu Parekh's admonition (see Chapter 4) that we should find ways of reconciling the legitimate demands of unity and diversity, of achieving unity without cultural uniformity, and cultivate among our members both a common sense of belonging and a willingness to respect and cherish deep cultural differences, is tested to the limit with issues such as this. Our cultural worldviews are challenged, a process which can be painful and takes time to work through, but each time of testing has the potential to leave us with a better understanding both of others and ourselves, and better equipped to engage with the world outside.

Mission as personal and church renewal

Leading a multicultural church requires a willingness to make space for all to participate in the life of the local church. In so doing the church as the people of God cannot be static, with little changing year on year. Instead it should become open to the renewing work of the Holy Spirit because of its commitment to grow as a multicultural community.

Rabbi Lord Jonathan Sacks, in his book *The Home We Build Together*, reflects on the significance of the building of the Tabernacle by the Israelites in the wilderness. He notes that the early part of the book of Exodus is all about 'the politics of freedom'. But he also observes that the last third of the book 'is taken up with an apparently minor and irrelevant episode told and retold in exhaustive detail: the construction of the Tabernacle' (Sacks, 2007, p. 136). Sacks queries why the story is told at such length and notes the linguistic parallels with the story of God's creation of the universe in Genesis. He goes on to assert that a nation does not just happen but has to be created: 'In commanding Moses to get the people to make the Tabernacle God was in effect saying: To turn a group of individuals into a covenantal nation, they must build something together' (Sacks, 2007, p. 137). He goes on to say:

Society is the home, the Tabernacle, we build together. It was built out of difference and diversity. That too is the point of the narrative . . . The Tabernacle was built out of the differential contributions of the various groups and tribes. It represented orchestrated diversity, or in social terms, integration without assimilation. That is the dignity of difference. Because we are not the same, we each have something unique to contribute, something only we can give.   (Sacks, 2007, p. 138)

Sacks is saying that a community does not just exist by virtue of a group of people coming together. It has to be built, with everyone playing their part, and it is in the process of construction that people are bound together, giving them a shared sense of ownership, belonging, and a place to call home. Through the act of building something together we become integrated, attached, and rooted into the community in which we participate.

The New Testament scholar Robert Banks, reflecting on the Greek term *koinonia*, notes that the word, often translated as 'fellowship', is taken to mean 'the sharing of people concerned directly with one another'. However, he states that it should be interpreted with the sense of 'participation in some common object or activity' (Banks, 1994, p. 57). This sense of participation echoes neatly the description of the Israelites building the Tabernacle together. It seems then that it is in this building together that a sense of ownership, fellowship and joy is generated.

Sociologist Zygmunt Bauman celebrates the possibilities that multicultural life can bring:

The pluralism of modern civilized society is not just a 'brute fact' which can be disliked or even detested but (alas) not wished away, but a good thing and fortunate circumstance, as it offers benefits much in excess of the discomforts and inconveniences it brings, widens horizons for humanity and multiplies the chances of life altogether more prepossessing than the conditions any of its alternatives may deliver.

(Bauman, 2000, p. 178)

A man from Sudan who had been attending a multicultural church for some time put it to me like this: 'every Sunday is like a stone, every Sunday I go there, and you know you are building something, you are putting a stone over a stone. Yes, I think it's a beautiful thing.'

If a commitment to develop multiculturally offers the potential to be renewed as a community, it also has the potential to lead to personal renewal as we make our own commitment to grow as individuals and as members of a multicultural church. My wife, who is of Jamaican descent, and I continually discover ways in which prejudice still lurks in our minds and our hearts. Discovering such prejudice, confessing it and overcoming it is part of our becoming more like Christ. We become better people, with purer hearts, in our relationships with all people.

Mission and church growth

There is a strong correlation between migration, the expansion of cities and growth in the number of multicultural churches. People migrate to cities to seek asylum, fleeing war-torn regions, to find work and improve their economic prospects, to study, to connect with family and to travel. According to the United Nations report *State of the World's Cities 2010/2011*, one in three people in the world lived in cities by the mid-twentieth century. In 2010 that had increased to half, and the number is expected to continue to grow to 70 per cent by 2050 (UN-HABITAT, 2008, p. 13). In the UK it was reported that by 2012, 54 per cent of the population were living in cities (Champion, 2014). Cities are by nature multicultural and they grow primarily as a result of migration, therefore bringing together in one place people from differing ethnic and cultural backgrounds. Such people interact in neighbourhoods, schools, places of work and churches. At a midweek gathering in my own church, of the 34 people present only four had been born in London. Some had migrated to London from other parts of the world, and some were white British people who had migrated to the city from other parts of the UK. Of the four who were born in London, two were white and two were black. The rapid growth of cities presents a new challenge for the Church in its mission to proclaim the gospel to the whole world, as the people we are seeking to reach will increasingly be found living in such places.

Multicultural churches have an advantage in their ability to reach multicultural communities. The diversity of people present in such a church enables its outreach into the local community to be more effective. Although many first-generation immigrants can be found in expatriate congregations, their children grow up in multicultural schools and universities and are often looking for multicultural congregations in which to worship, and within which, in time, to raise their own children. It is not unusual for parents with young children who start coming to our church to say that they wanted a multicultural church to belong to. This becomes a strong attracting factor even if other things, such as the style of worship, are not as they would wish. A significant proportion of these second-generation immigrants are finding partners of a different ethnic back-ground from their own and are thus raising children of mixed heritage. Statistics show that the percentage of people in the UK belonging to ethnic minorities grew from 9 per cent to 14 per cent between 2001 and 2011, but within this figure, the percentage of those describing themselves as of mixed ethnicity doubled, making them the fastest rising ethnic minority cate-gory in the UK and increasing the relevance of multicultural churches to the changing demographic.

In 1970 missiologist Donald McGavran published a seminal work, *Understanding Church Growth*, in which he argued:

It takes no great acumen to see that when marked differences of color, stature, income, cleanliness, and education are present . . . [human beings] understand the Gospel better when expounded by their own kind of people. They prefer to join churches whose members look, talk, and act like themselves.

(McGavran, 1970, p. 198)

McGavran's argument was that the most effective way to reach people with the gospel was to do so by targeting specific people groups and establishing churches that people could more readily identify with. He insisted that evangelism would be made more effective by application of what has been known since as the 'homogeneous unit principle'. Although in advocating the development of multicultural churches the argument of the present book flows against this principle, it is notable that some of the fastest growing churches numerically in the UK are black-majority churches.

Mark Sturge urges caution when applying the label 'homogeneous' to black-majority churches. He points out that African and Caribbean churches are more ethnically diverse than they may appear, as the people within them, though labelled 'African', are in fact from many different nations and tribal groups within the continent (Sturge, 2005, p. 41). Of course, to some extent all churches create spaces for like-minded people to gather (for example youth groups, women's groups), and certainly the prevalence of expatriate congregations in the UK shows the ease with which such an approach aids the evangelism, discipleship and pastoral care of such communities as they establish themselves in a strange land. The Church of England report *Mission-shaped Church* supports McGavran's notion of a 'culture-specific social expression of the gospel' in certain circumstances, where it is desirable to bridge the gap to cultures which have proved difficult to reach by conventional approaches to mission. But the report also recognizes that the idea of purposefully pursuing the creation of homogeneous churches as an effective means of evangelism has attracted much criticism.[1]

Israel Olafinjana, Baptist minister and author, considers the impact of West African-led churches in the UK. After reviewing the impact and legacy of Europeans in the 'dark continent of Africa' he goes on to review the impact and legacy of more recent developments resulting from the arrival of West Africans in the 'dark continent of Europe'. His argument is that the rise of the African-led churches has been a major feature which counters the decline of the Church in Europe, what is described as 'the reverse flow in missions from South to North' (Olafinjana, 2010, p. 48). He notes that some of the largest churches in the UK which have experienced significant numerical growth are African-led, and have several characteristics in common: strong leadership; a high level of faith expectation; the communal nature of black culture, which goes beyond Sunday services; a holistic approach to mission, caring for every aspect of a person's life; prosperity theology, which addresses the socio-economic needs of migrant communities; being a social hub for new migrants; a dynamic style of worship; high levels of financial commitment; the use of media and professionally printed advertising; a high commitment to prayer and fasting; and confident engagement with the spirit world, which is considered more seriously within West African cultures than in the West (Olafinjana, 2010, pp. 52–3).

Olafinjana also lists what he sees as the weaknesses of these African-led churches: the lack of cross-cultural mission strategies; the unhealthy extremes to which prosperity theology is taken; and a lack of unity between Afro-Caribbean churches, of contextualization of African forms of Christianity within British culture, of theological education, of ecumenical partnership with churches of other origins, and of political engagement (Olafinjana, 2010, pp. 56–7). It is notable that he perceives the lack of integration of these churches, in a number of different ways, to be a weakness in their ability to sustain their growth and development as mission churches in the UK. These churches will ultimately need to extend their multicultural composition to embrace those of other continents and worldviews if they are to continue to increase their reach.

Ecuadorian theologian René Padilla takes issue with McGavran, offering five reasons to reject his theory. Drawing from an exegetical analysis of the New Testament, Padilla argues that Jews and Gentiles heard the gospel together; that breaking down the barriers that separate people was an essential aspect of the gospel; that the Church grew across cultural barriers; that each church 'was meant to portray the oneness of its members regardless of their racial, cultural, or social differences'; and that Christian community across cultural barriers was 'essential to Christian commitment' (Padilla, 1982, p. 29). Craig Keener agrees with Padilla when he writes, 'Paul demanded ethnic unity in Christ as an integral part of the gospel he preached' (Keener, 2003, p. 213). Whether we are thinking of existing churches or planting new churches in multicultural communities, then the development of multicultural churches should be part of any denomination or church network's mission strategy in the UK today.

Given the challenge of mission in the UK at the present time, we have explored in this chapter the ways that a multicultural church can extend the kingdom of God within the community to which it seeks to witness. Through unity, justice, renewal and church growth, multicultural churches can continue to thrive and strengthen, becoming a foretaste of heaven on earth. Indeed, as the world becomes increasingly urban and cities grow ever larger, such churches may prove to be the new frontier of mission in the decades to come.

Conclusion to Part 2

In Part 1 of this book, I laid out three key foundations for the development of a biblical perspective on multicultural church, drawing attention to Bhikhu Parekh's encouragement to strive for unity without uniformity, and finding in Gordon Allport's research a framework to assist us in overcoming prejudice. However, the real test comes when one begins to implement such thinking in everyday church life. In Part 2 I have sought to build on these foundations, considering how, in a myriad of ways, we may begin to implement change. Success in developing a healthy multicultural environment will come not so much from a few big changes but more likely from a great many small ones, reflecting a subtle shift towards being an instinctively inclusive congregation.

Worship (Chapter 6) is an area which will take much thought and preparation, if we are to find achievable ways to include the contributions of everyone in the congregation, and develop liturgies that reflect the whole people of God. Navigating through the pastoral challenges (Chapter 7), we recognized some of the difficulties and potential pitfalls involved in leading a multicultural church. Garces-Foley's description of a multicultural church as a culture of discomfort will resonate with many. The ability to facilitate a level of fellowship and friendship across cultures to mitigate and overcome such discomfort is key.

Developing diverse leadership teams (Chapter 8) may well prove to be the most important chapter in this part of the book. Empowering people of different ethnic and cultural backgrounds to participate within multicultural teams is what will ensure that the changes we make are not superficial. Hofstede's dimensions of culture may help us to analyse and overcome some of the difficulties that can arise in committees or leadership teams.

Finally, our consideration of aspects of mission reminds us that to become a healthy, growing, multicultural church is not an end in itself; its purpose is to serve the kingdom of God, in these changing times, more effectively. I hope this book may help all of those in church leadership in multicultural communities to believe that developing healthy, growing, multi-cultural congregations is an aim that is desirable, beneficial and achievable.

Notes

1 Introduction

1 Figures taken from the report *Dynamics of Diversity, Evidence from the 2011 Census*, published by the Centre on Dynamics of Ethnicity, accessed at <www.ethnicity.ac.uk/medialibrary/briefings/dynamicsofdiversity/how-has-ethnic-diversity-grown-1991-2001-2011.pdf>, 22 February 2016.

2 Figures taken from the *English Church Census 2005*, accessed at <http://www.eauk.org/church/research-and-statistics/english-church-census.cfm>, 22 February 2016.

2 Thinking biblically about multicultural church: Old Testament

1 Others include K. E. Bailey, *Jesus Through Middle Eastern Eyes* (London: SPCK, London, 2008); A. L. Nieves (ed.), *The Latino Heritage Bible* (Iowa: World Bible Pub., 2002); and C. H. Felder (ed.), *The Original African Heritage Study Bible* (Iowa: World Bible Pub., 1998).

2 This reflects the stance of the *Africa Bible Commentary*, which describes its approach as such: 'While remaining true to the biblical text, it must apply biblical teachings and truths to African realities' (Adeyemo, 2006, p. ix).

3 See also Brueggemann, 2009, p. 102. For discussion of difficulties with Genesis 10 see Hays, 2003, pp. 58–9.

4 Others have suggested on linguistic grounds that Abraham originates from the Amorites; see Hays, 2003, p. 32.

5 See discussion in D. T. Olsen, *Numbers* (Louisville: John Knox Press, 1996), pp. 70–1 regarding differing views on who Moses married and where his wife came from. Following P. J. Budd, *Numbers* (Waco: Word, 1984), p. 136, I take the view that Moses married a Cushite woman, and that the Cushites came from the Nubian region south of Egypt which was also synonymous with

Ethiopia at the time. Yamauchi, after surveying the archaeological and historical evidence, states that 'we should not doubt the possibility of Moses' marriage to a Kushite or Nubian woman' (Yamauchi, 2004, p. 75).

6 See also Preuss, 1996, p. 292.

7 See also Isaiah 56.8; 60.3, 7, 10–14; Zechariah 8.20–23.

8 See also Isaiah 19.19–21; 42.6; 49.6; Zephaniah 2.11.

9 'Rahab' is used in this psalm as an epithet for Egypt (Tate, 1990, p. 391).

10 J. P. Burnside also notes two other categories, the *toshav*, which is synonymous with *ger*, and the *nokri*, who 'is the foreigner who lives in his own country outside of Israel'. J. P. Burnside, *The Status and Welfare of Immigrants* (Cambridge: The Jubilee Centre, 2001), pp. 16–17.

11 Note that there is variation among scholars regarding the dating of Deuteronomy. P. C. Craigie, *Deuteronomy* (Grand Rapids: Eerdmans, 1976), pp. 24–9 argues for a much earlier date, Preuss, 1996, p. 289 for a post-exilic date.

12 Tigay, 1996, p. 479 suggests that a list such as Ammonites, Moabites, Edomites and Egyptians effectively refers to all foreigners (cf. J. Goldingay, *Old Testament Theology*, Vol. 3 (Downers Grove: IVP, 2009, p. 510), but that suggestion is undermined by the specific exemption offered to descendants of Edom and Egypt.

13 McConville also draws attention to the covenant made with the Gibeonites in Joshua 9.

14 The Rt Revd Dr James Jones, Bishop of Liverpool, extract from his lecture 'The Moral of this Story? Jesus', given as the last of a series of four in October 2001 as The London Lectures in Contemporary Christianity.

3 Thinking biblically about multicultural church: New Testament

1 For a contrary view suggesting that the inclusion of the four women is unrelated to their foreignness as each had proselytized, see J. Nolland, *Matthew* (Grand Rapids: Eerdmans, 2005), pp. 75–6.

2 See discussion in Hays, 2003, pp. 164–5 regarding the likeliness of these allusions. Hays concludes (p. 165), 'It is the overall theme of Genesis 10—12, not just a reversal of the Tower of Babel, that is important to Luke.'

3 See also D. E. Aune, *Revelation 1—5* (Dallas: Word, 1997), p. 362. Aune quotes Origen, Justin, Diognetus and Tertullian among the early Christian writers who used this designation.

4 The phrase 'all nations and people of every language' also appears in various forms in Daniel 3.4, 7, 29; 5.19; 6.25; 7.14; Revelation 5.9; 10.11; 11.9; 13.7; 17.15.

6 Approaches to worship

1 A Prayer for the Refugee Crisis, <www.churchofengland.org/prayer-worship/topical-prayers/a-prayer-for-the-refugee-crisis.aspx>, accessed 6 February 2016.

8 Developing diverse leadership teams

1 Two further dimensions (long-term versus short-term and self-discipline) were subsequently added by Hofstede; they have not been included for discussion here but the reader may wish to refer to them.

9 Growing in mission

1 Discussed in *Mission-shaped Church – Church Planting and Fresh Expressions of Church in a Changing Context*, report published by The Archbishops' Council (Church House Publishing, 2004), pp. 108–9.

References

1 Introduction

Karlsen, S., and Nazroo, J. Y., 'Defining and measuring ethnicity and "race": theoretical & conceptual issues for health & social care research', in Nazroo, J. Y., ed. (2006), *Health and Social Research in Multi-Ethnic Societies*, Oxford: Routledge.

Parekh, B., 'What is Multiculturalism?' from www.india-seminar.com, 1999, accessed 13 September 2006.

2 Thinking biblically about multicultural church: Old Testament

Adeyemo, T., ed. (2006), *Africa Bible Commentary*, Grand Rapids: Zondervan.

Anderson, B. W. (1994), *From Creation to New Creation*, Minneapolis: Fortress Press.

Bright, J. (1981), *A History of Israel*, 3rd edn, London: SCM Press.

Brueggemann, W. (1982), *Genesis*, Atlanta: John Knox Press.

Brueggemann, W. (1994), *Exodus*, Nashville: Abingdon Press.

Brueggemann, W. (1997), *Theology of the Old Testament*, Minneapolis: Fortress Press.

Brueggemann, W. (2009), *An Unsettling God*, Minneapolis: Fortress Press.

Childs, B. S. (2001), *Isaiah*, Louisville: John Knox Press.

Clements, R. E. (1998), 'Deuteronomy' in *NIB* Vol. II, Nashville: Abingdon Press.

Durham, J. I. (1987), *Exodus*, Waco: Word.

Erskine, N. L. (1998), *Decolonizing Theology*, New Jersey: Africa World Press.

Felder, C. H., ed. (1991), *Stony the Road We Trod*, Minneapolis: Fortress Press.

France, R. T. (2002), *The Gospel of Mark*, Carlisle: Paternoster Press.

References

Franks, M. C. (1998), 'Election, Pluralism, and the Missiology of Scripture in a Postmodern Age', *Missiology: An International Review*, July.

Hamilton, V. P. (1990), *Genesis 1—17*, Grand Rapids: Eerdmans.

Hamilton, V. P. (1995), *Genesis 18—50*, Grand Rapids: Eerdmans,.

Hays, J. D. (2003), *From Every People and Nation*, Leicester: Apollos.

Lane, W. L. (1974), *The Gospel of Mark*, Grand Rapids: Eerdmans.

McConville, J. G., and Williams, S. N. (2010), *Joshua*, Cambridge: Eerdmans.

Mays, J. L. (1994), *Psalms*, Louisville: John Knox Press.

Preuss, H. D. (1996), *Old Testament Theology*, Vol. II, Edinburgh: Westminster John Knox Press.

Routledge, R. (2008), *Old Testament Theology*, Nottingham: Apollos.

Sanneh, L. (2009), *Translating the Message*, 2nd edn, Maryknoll: Orbis.

Sarna, N. M. (1991), *Exodus*, New York: Jewish Publication Society.

Schniedewind, W. M. (2002), 'The Rise of the Aramean States' in M. W. Chavalas and K. L. Younger Jr (eds), *Mesopotamia and the Bible*, Grand Rapids: Baker Academic.

Tate, M. E. (1990), *Psalms 51—100*, Dallas: Word.

Tennent, T. C. (2007), *Theology in the Context of World Christianity*, Grand Rapids: Zondervan.

Thiessen, M. (2009), 'The Function of a Conjunction: Inclusivist or Exclusivist Strategies in Ezra 6.19–21 and Nehemiah 10.29–30?', *JSOT* 34.1.

Tigay, J. H. (1996), *Deuteronomy*, Philadelphia: Jewish Publication Society.

Usry, G., and Keener, C. S. (1996), *Black Man's Religion*, Downers Grove: IVP.

Van De Mieroop, M. (2004), *A History of the Ancient Near East*, Oxford: Blackwell.

Von Rad, G. (1972), *Genesis OTL*, 3rd edn, London: SCM Press.

Walls, A. F. (2002), *The Cross-cultural Process in Christian History*, New York: Orbis.

Weiser, A. (1962), *The Psalms*, London: SCM Press.

Wenham, G. J. (1987), *Genesis 1—15*, Waco: Word.

Westermann, C. (2004), *Genesis*, London: T&T Clark.

Williamson Jr, L. (1983), *Mark*, Atlanta: John Knox Press.

Wright, C. J. H. (2006), *The Mission of God*, Nottingham: IVP.

Yamauchi, E. M. (2004), *Africa and the Bible*, Grand Rapids: Baker Academic.

3 Thinking biblically about multicultural church: New Testament

Beale, G. K. (1999), *The Book of Revelation*, Carlisle: Paternoster Press.

Boyarin, D. (1994), *A Radical Jew: Paul and the Politics of Identity*, London: University of California Press.

Carson, D. (1991), *The Gospel According to John*, Leicester: IVP.

Cousar, C. B. (1982), *Galatians*, Atlanta: John Knox Press.

Cousar, C. B. (1998), 'Paul and Multiculturalism' in W. Brueggemann and G. W. Stroup (eds), *Many Voices One God*, Louisville: John Knox Press.

France, R. T. (2007), *Matthew*, Grand Rapids: Eerdmans.

Hays, J. D. (2003), *From Every People and Nation*, Leicester: Apollos.

Hoehner, H. W. (2002), *Ephesians*, Grand Rapids: Baker Academic.

Johnson, L. T. (1992), *The Acts of the Apostles*, Collegeville: The Liturgical Press.

Keener, C. S. (2003), 'Some New Testament Invitations to Ethnic Reconciliation', *Evangelical Quarterly*, Carlisle: Paternoster, July.

LaGrand, L. (1999), *The Earliest Christian Mission to 'All Nations' in the Light of Matthew's Gospel*, 2nd edn, Grand Rapids: Eerdmans.

Lane, W. L. (1974), *The Gospel of Mark*, Grand Rapids: Eerdmans.

McEvedy, C. (2002), *The New Penguin Atlas of Ancient History*, 2nd edn, London: Penguin Books.

Milne, B. (2007), *Dynamic Diversity*, Downers Grove: IVP.

Peterson, D. G. (2009), *The Acts of the Apostles*, Nottingham: Apollos.

Wright, C. J. H. (2006), *The Mission of God*, Nottingham: IVP.

Yamauchi, E. M. (2004), *Africa and the Bible*, Grand Rapids: Baker Academic.

4 Multiculturalism in context

Barry, B. (2001), *Culture and Equality*, Cambridge: Polity Press.

Brah, A. (2007), 'Non-binarized Identities of Similarity and Difference' in *Identity, Ethnic Diversity and Community Cohesion*, London: Sage.

Jolley, A. (2015), *Growing Leaders from Diverse Cultures*, Cambridge: Grove Books.

Kymlicka, W. (2007), *Multicultural Odysseys*, Oxford: OUP.

Parekh, B. (1999), 'What is Multiculturalism?' from www.india-seminar. com, accessed 13 September 2006.

Parekh, B. (2000), *Rethinking Multiculturalism*, Basingstoke: Palgrave.

Parekh, B. (2008), *A New Politics of Identity*, Basingstoke: Palgrave Macmillan.

Tebble, A. J. (2006), 'Exclusion for Democracy', *Political Theory* 34, London: Sage.

5 Overcoming prejudice

Allport, G. W. (1979), *The Nature of Prejudice*, 25th anniversary edn, New York: Basic Books.

Garner, S., et al. (2009), *Sources of Resentment, and Perceptions of Ethnic Minorities among Poor White People in England*, report compiled for the National Community Forum, London: Department for Communities and Local Government.

6 Approaches to worship

The Archbishops' Council (2015), *Reflections for Daily Prayer: Advent 2015 to Eve of Advent 2016*, London: Church House Publishing.

Baker, J. (2010), *Curating Worship*, London: SPCK.

Bowers, L. B. (2006), *Becoming a Multicultural Church*, Cleveland: The Pilgrim Press.

Carvalhaes, C. (2011), 'Communitas: liturgy and identity', *International Review of Mission* 100.1, April.

DeYmaz, M. (2007), *Building a Healthy Multi-ethnic Church*, San Francisco: Jossey Bass.

Ellis, C. (2009), *Approaching God*, London: Canterbury Press.

Jolley, A. (2015), *Growing Leaders from Diverse Cultures*, Cambridge: Grove Books.

Law, E. H. F. (1993), *The Wolf Shall Dwell with the Lamb*, St Louis: Chalice Press.

Mitchell, H. H. (1990), *Black Preaching*, Nashville: Abingdon Press.

Parekh, B. (1999), 'What is Multiculturalism?' from www.india-seminar.com, accessed 13 September 2006.

Reddie, A. G., *Is God Colour-blind?* London: SPCK, 2009.

Sandiford, D. (2010), *Multiethnic Church*, Cambridge: Grove Books.

Sturge, M. (2005), *Look What the Lord has Done!*, Bletchley: Scripture Union.

Tarrant, I. (2012), *Worship and Freedom in the Church of England*, Cambridge: Grove Books.

7 Navigating the pastoral challenges

Bauman, Z. (2000), *Liquid Modernity*, Cambridge: Polity Press.

Garces-Foley, K. (2007), *Crossing the Ethnic Divide*, New York: OUP.

Jagessar, M. N. (2011), *United Reformed Church Mission Council Report May 2011*, London: URC.

Jolley, A. (2015), *Growing Leaders from Diverse Cultures*, Cambridge: Grove Books.

Sandiford, D. (2010), *Multiethnic Church*, Cambridge: Grove Books.

Stanley, B. (2009), *The World Missionary Conference, Edinburgh 1910*, Cambridge: Eerdmans.

Volf, M. (1996), *Exclusion and Embrace*, Nashville: Abingdon Press.

Washington, R., and Kehrein, G. (1993), *Breaking Down Walls*, Chicago: Moody Press.

8 Developing diverse leadership teams

Hofstede, G., Hofstede, G. and Minkov, M. (2010), *Cultures and Organizations*, London: McGraw Hill.

Jolley, A. (2015), *Growing Leaders from Diverse Cultures*, Cambridge: Grove Books.

Sandiford, D. (2010), *Multiethnic Church*, Cambridge: Grove Books.

9 Growing in mission

The Archbishops' Council Report (2004), *Mission-shaped Church*, London: Church House Publishing.

Banks, R. (1994), *Paul's Idea of Community*, Peabody: Hendrickson.

Bauman, Z. (2000) *Liquid Modernity*, Cambridge: Polity Press.

Champion, T. (2014), 'People in Cities: The Numbers', report commissioned by the Government Office for Science, UK, June.

Keener, C. S. (2003), 'Some New Testament Invitations to Ethnic Reconciliation', *Evangelical Quarterly*, Carlisle: Paternoster, July.

McGavran, D. A. (1970), *Understanding Church Growth*, Grand Rapids: Eerdmans.

McLaren, B., Padilla, E., and Seeber, A. B. (2009), *The Justice Project*, Grand Rapids: Baker Books.

Olafinjana, I. (2010), *Reverse in Ministry and Missions: Africans in the Dark Continent of Europe*, Milton Keynes: AuthorHouse.

Padilla, C. R. (1982), 'The Unity of the Church and the Homogeneous Unit Principle', *International Bulletin of Mission Research*, January.

Peskett, H., and Ramachandra, V. (2003), *The Message of Mission*, Leicester: IVP.

Rajagopalan, K. (2010), 'What is the Defining Divide?', *Black Theology*, August.

Sacks, J. (2007), *The Home We Build Together*, London: Continuum.

Storkey, E. (2015), *Scars Across Humanity*, London: SPCK.

Sturge, M. (2005), *Look What the Lord Has Done!*, Bletchley: Scripture Union.

UN-HABITAT Report (2008), *State of the World's Cities 2010/2011*, UN Human Settlements Programme.

Index of Scripture references

Index of authors

Index of subjects

Index of subjects